GOD COLLARED

GOD COLLARED

By
JAMES MARTIN

First edition published 1992 by Chapter House Ltd
26 Bothwell Street, Glasgow G2 6PA.

ISBN 0-948643-08-0

Typeset by Nuprint Ltd., Harpenden
Printed in the UK by Bell and Bain Ltd, Glasgow

Dedication

This book is dedicated to
those many ministers who through the years have
shown graciousness in ways large and small
to this fellow-minister.

Contents

Introduction

THE LAST THING I WANTED

FTER I HAD DECIDED that I should become a minister, my mother was heard to say, 'I think Jim was always meant to be a minister. He was always pretending to be one when he was a small boy.'

She was perfectly correct about my small boy antics. To my present embarrassment I remember only too well how in those now far-off days of my early childhood I used to stand in front of our wardrobe mirror and preach endless sermons to an imaginary (fortunately) congregation, and occasionally managed to press-gang my two nearest brothers (poor souls) to make up a live audience. I revelled in this bit of play-acting, conceited little pup that I must have been. I revelled also in the indulgent comments that adults were prone to make of this behaviour (although no doubt thinking at the same time, 'what an obnoxious child') such as 'I wouldn't be surprised if he does go into the ministry some day.' And I sometimes found myself thinking 'I would really enjoy being a minister,' even though at my then tender age of seven or eight I was not what you might call very conversant with what being a minister entailed.

None of this, however, had the slightest influence on my eventually deciding to offer myself for the ministry. When it came to the point of decision, in fact, being a minister was far from being something I thought I would enjoy. Truth to tell, it was about the last thing that at that stage I *wanted* to be.

When I first began to hear God's voice calling me to the

ministry, calling more and more insistently as I sat Sunday morning by Sunday morning in Manse Road Church, Motherwell, along with my Boys' Brigade contemporaries, I was able to think of a host of other things I would prefer to do with my life and I was able, too, to think of just as many good reasons for recoiling from any thoughts of the ministry.

Nor was there anything in my background to suggest that I was a likely prospect for the ministry of the church. There had been no ministers in our family either on my father's or my mother's side. Financially we were in such poor circumstances as made University education an unlikely line for any of the family to follow in those pre-state grant days.

On the other hand I had a decidedly Christian upbringing and that may well have been the factor that was decisive in the end.

When my publisher suggested entitling this book *Marvellous Ministry* to reflect the belief underlying it that being a minister of the church is a marvellous job, I was fearful that such a title might seem to be a claim that my own ministry had been marvellous in terms of success. Whereas, much more than its apparent successes, I am mindful of its deficiencies—things I wish I had done, things I wish I had not done, things I wish I had done better. So we settled in the end on *God Collared*, a title that indicates my conviction that it was not so much that I chose the ministry as that God chose me for it. I hope, nevertheless, that the following pages reflect clearly that in my experience the ministry, in spite of all else, *is* marvellous.

Chapter One

'Revving Up' In Childhood

WHEN IN MY RETIREMENT I look back over my life, I find it extremely difficult to conceive of myself as filling any role other than that of a minister of the Gospel. In that sense, I suppose, it could be said that I was always destined for the Church.

My childhood, however, gave little indication that this was a foregone conclusion—often quite the reverse. At the same time it would be foolish and wrong to suggest that my childhood made no contribution to the minister I was to become. Everyone is indebted for good or ill to his or her past, even the earliest past, and I can see clearly, looking back, that I was no exception to the rule.

My eventual donning of the 'dog collar' undoubtedly owed much to my being brought up in a Christian home. I was richly blessed in my parents. My mother was devout in an unostentatious way and a regular churchgoer; and although my father was the kind of run-of-the-mill Church of Scotland member who takes good care not to let himself go overboard about his faith, from my earliest memory I lived in an atmosphere of Christian belief and practice.

The atmosphere was one of happiness, too, despite the fact that we were anything but well off. I was the first-born of a family which in the end consisted of six boys. My father, who had been badly wounded in the First World War but like many another had returned to the front after a period of recovery and convalescence, went back on demobilisation to his job in the local steelworks of Colvilles. Immediately post-war times were hard for most people, however, and became harder as the years passed. Our family suffered with the majority.

I can still remember the pain of the shame I felt in my early schooldays (which I now realise must have been only a fraction of that which my proud parents experienced) when they had to take me to Marshall's boot and shoe shop to be fitted out with a pair of 'parish boots'. Young though I was, the hurt went very deep, especially since I was well aware that everyone knew these ugly 'tacketty' boots for the charity hand-out that they were; and schoolmates were not slow to jibe and to jeer at the wearer of them. The only slight compensating factor was the ability of the 'tackets' to strike a stream of sparks from the pavement if the proper contact was made.

The depth of that hurt is matched in my memory by the mortification of having, on another occasion, to return to my schoolteacher and confess that my mother simply did not have the penny I was expected, along with the rest of the class, to take to school so that I might take home as my very own the calendar I had made in class.

There was certainly no thought in anyone's mind then that I would one day be a minister of the kirk. Nevertheless, I suppose, these experiences played their part in the preparation of what was to be; and, I suppose also, so did most of the experiences which my memory plucks out of these now distant years.

For one thing, I learned early that life is not always fair. True, I learned the lesson in what I now recognise to have been a gentle fashion, although embittering enough at the time, but I learned it clearly all the same. I was the eldest of six sons who came, as it were, in two batches of three. The two others in my group were closer in age to each other than to me with the perhaps inevitable result that they tended often to gang up on me. This was frequently so in bed at night. In our younger years we slept in the same bed in what was termed in our stratum of society 'the room' in our two apartment home. As the eldest, I slept at the front of the bed with the others between me and the wall. One of their regular ploys was to combine forces to push me forcibly out of bed and on to the floor, usually with a resounding bump that brought my father hastening through to see what was amiss. Invariably I was the one who received any rebuke or punishment that might ensue. Just as invariably when I attempted to protest my innocence, my father simply continued with whatever chastisement he was administering, saying, 'You are the oldest and ought therefore to know better'. The injustice of it all rankled then and is still remembered.

It was, too, in those early days that my passion for the game of football taught me not only that one cannot expect always to be on the winning side but also the parallel lesson that sometimes even winning can carry its problems.

I was, at nine years of age, captain of our street team of boys around the same age. This, I must confess, was not because I was the best player in the group—I was far from being that, although not, I think, the worst either—but for a much more potent reason. I was the owner of the ball, a genuine leather football. I did not have any more money than the rest as we were all in the same impoverished boat; but I had been fortunate enough to win the ball as a prize in a competition run by my weekly boys' magazine, *The Rover*.

One summer evening we had a challenge match in opposition to our bitter rivals from a nearby street and the match was played in the public park about a mile away.

They were a good team and proud of never having tasted defeat so far that summer. When we triumphed by two goals to one they were extremely displeased. Suddenly the desire for revenge proved too much for one of their boys and he let out a shout, "Come on. Let's burst their ball'. When I heard that shout and saw them turning in a body towards me, my heart leaped with fright. I grabbed the ball tightly to my chest and took to my heels, as did the rest of my team, with the opposing team in feverish pursuit, screaming threats all the while. I had never run so fast in all my life nor had I ever felt such panic. Somehow I made it home with both myself and the ball still intact—but we took good care never to play that team again.

Football played a large part in my childhood life and very nearly was the cause of me never progressing beyond childhood. It was in that same nine year old period that our school football team—every one of whose matches I had attended with increasingly fervid support—had reached the final of the Motherwell Primary Schools Cup. The match was to take place on the ground of Motherwell Juniors F.C. and, like many other boys in the school, I was given a batch of tickets to sell for it. I had already succeeded in disposing of quite a number when I called on one neighbour who was, I knew, certain to buy a ticket. When I was told that he was at that very moment in a shop on the other side of the main street, I was too impatient to wait for his return in case some other vendor should get to him first. I decided I must get to him as quickly as possible and go across to the shop after him. In my haste I rushed off the pavement without looking either to right or to left and the next instant I was lying spread-eagled on the road. I had run straight into the path of an oncoming cyclist. As I lay there, dazed and bleeding from head and leg, I heard a frantic squealing of brakes and could just catch sight of a bus towering above me—to my childish gaze it seemed as high as a mountain—and I was sure I was going to be killed. There seemed no way that the bus could stop in time, but it did.

I was patched up—stitched and bandaged, with nothing broken—and in a day or two was able to return to school. To my surprise I found myself something of a mini-hero. The whole school seemed to know that Jim Martin had been knocked down in the cause of selling tickets for the final. When the evening of the match arrived, I was still hobbling pretty badly and was still bandaged head and leg. Because of this I was given a VIP seat beside the teachers in the little wooden erection that served as a grandstand. But despite the flattering attention I was receiving and the sweets that were being passed to me, I knew that I would be enjoying the game even more if I were standing alongside my chums. What is more, the team obviously needed my support nearer the field of play as by half-time they had not yet scored. Accordingly, at the half-time interval I forsook my exalted position and went down to join my colleagues, temporary cripple though I was. How well I enjoyed the second half and how well did my boyish strategy work. Our team won by three goals to one.

That experience which could so easily have been fatal, gave me even at that early age an awareness of the frailty of human life which has been with me ever since. It also made me ever afterwards exceedingly careful crossing the street, and that, too, was no bad lesson to learn.

As a child I had an intense belief in Santa Claus which survived until the relatively far advanced age of eight or so. A considerable number of pundits would probably find it surprising that, in spite of that, I should develop a real Christian faith and even enter the ministry. Many consider that a belief in Santa Claus can only be harmful so far as Christian faith is concerned. It carries with it, they maintain, the risk that when children discover the deception, they may discard for ever the Gospel story as belonging to the same school of childish fantasy.

All I can say is that it did not work like that with me. Admittedly, it was a shock when I discovered that Santa Claus was, in fact, no other than my loving parents but I do not believe the experience made it any more difficult for me to believe in the Christian faith. I recall only the sheer joy which Santa added to my first Christmasses.

It was in those now far-off days, to change the subject, that I first felt the burden of a sense of sin. I was a regular attender of Sunday School. My parents saw to that. My bosom pal, Jimmy Hunter, was not. One Sunday afternoon on my way to Sunday School, I met in with Jimmy and he

"Our team won by three goals to one"

walked with me till we were within sight of the church. There he suggested that it was a shame to go in there out of the sunshine and I finished by truanting and spending my offering penny on sweets. But I felt miserable and never repeated the exercise. I do not doubt that that experience is rightly counted as part of my spiritual enlightenment and theological development, even if at the time my reaction may have been occasioned only by fear that my parents would find out what I had done. So, too, no doubt was my early experience of private prayer. In my early boyhood I looked on prayer more or less as a kind of order form made out verbally to a divine Santa Claus who could be depended on to attend to it faithfully and without fail. Most of my early boyhood prayers were requests for my beloved Motherwell Football Club to win Saturday afternoon by Saturday afternoon. In those halcyon days when the Motherwell team was a mighty power in the land, they nearly always did win and this rather served to confirm me in my quite unscriptural view of prayer.

It was when I discovered, painfully, that my prayers were not always followed by a Motherwell victory that I was forced to a reappraisal of prayer's nature and function. To begin with I used to conclude that there must have been something in my prayer that was deficient when defeat came—perhaps it had been too short, or too casual, or not passionate enough—or something deficient in me personally. But gradually I came to realise that the simple explanation was that prayer was never intended to be the infallible request-granting system I had been trying to make it, but had a much wider and deeper significance.

My fanatical interest in football and in Motherwell F.C. in particular had one unfortunate result in those early days which ought to have taught me a lesson, too, although I doubt if it did. I somehow got myself enlisted in the little group of Manse Road Sunday School Scholars who had volunteered to compete in the National Bible Examination. We were prepared—and prepared marvellously well, I recall—by one of the Sunday School staff, Mrs Russell, who took us over all the prescribed Bible passages.

I found myself enjoying her weekly preparation classes and I also found that, as a result, I was assimilating the prescribed passages remarkably well. Then came a shock. I discovered that the examination, a written one, was to be held on a Saturday afternoon. Now, Saturday afternoons were when the Scottish football matches were played and I never went anywhere on a Saturday afternoon except to Fir Park to see Motherwell F.C. Mark you, the first team were away from home on that particular Saturday but the reserve team had a match at home—against Queen's Park Strollers—and the thought of missing even that was almost more than I could bear.

I could not get out of sitting the examination—much as I now wanted to—but I worked it out that if I got through it quickly enough I could get to the ground in time for the second half. The result was that when the day came, I raced through the exam at top speed and took my paper out to the presiding official fully thirty minutes before the scheduled end. 'Wouldn't you like to take some time to read it through before you hand in your paper?' she asked, 'Just in case you've missed something'.

'No, no' replied bighead 'I've done it all'.

But I had not. In my hurry I had completely omitted half a question. In consequence I scored 89% and came second in Scotland for my particular age group when if I had not been so besotted over an unimportant football match, I might well have been first and given so much additional pleasure to Mrs Russell as well as to my parents. It was a sharp lesson in the importance of getting things into their true perspective and yet I am only too well aware that, given the same set of circumstances, I might well have been as foolish again!

It was at an even more tender age that I came to discover with surprise and shock the wide gulf that existed between Protestants and Catholics so far as the Motherwell of that day was concerned. I was walking along the street heading homewards one day when a group of boys not much older than myself came running towards me. Suddenly I found myself surrounded and the leader said to me, 'Are you a Billy or a Dan?'

The question was totally incomprehensible to me and I made no reply. The question was repeated, even more aggressively, and this time I managed to stutter, 'I don't know.'

'You must be a Billy, then' cried another of the group, 'Well, we're Dans and we're going to show you what we think of Billys.' Whereupon a few of them cuffed me about the head and ears and rushed off, shouting delightedly, leaving me in a flood of tears. When I reached home, my father explained to me that Billy was a term for a Protestant and a Dan was a Catholic.

Up till then I had been sheltered to some extent, I suppose, from the Catholic/Protestant divide in the West of Scotland by virtue of the fact that my mother was English-born of a Yorkshire mother and was herself a stranger to the suspicion and hostility which were common on both sides of that divide. One incidental bonus of my mother's background so far as my brothers and I were concerned was that Christmas always was highlighted. It is really only since the end of the Second World War that Christmas has come to be universally celebrated in Scotland at large. I remember my father telling me that he as a child hung up his stocking not on Christmas Eve but on New Year's Eve and that this was how it was with nearly all of the children in Motherwell of his age group.

The supplanting of New Year by Christmas both as a social and as a religious celebration in Scotland was in the main a post-war phenomenon. Some people still incline to the opinion that it was a regrettable change but I am certainly not one of them. I rejoice that we have now so many Christmas Eve and Christmas Day church services, for instance, events which were virtually unknown in my youth. Owing to my mother's influence, Christmas was always for us a season of prime importance both for the giving and receiving of presents and for the Bethlehem story; and I am most grateful for that. From a very early age Christmas created in my heart and mind a sense of wonder which has never gone away and which, far from putting me off the Christian faith, surely helped prepare the way for my accepting it. Not least because my mother slaved and sacrificed to give us boys as good a Christmas as she could. Poor in material goods, she was abundantly rich in love.

It was also in those days of early childhood that I was given a lesson in the importance of tact and diplomacy, something perhaps not greatly expected of a ten year old boy, as I was at the time, but essential in the exercise of a pastoral ministry. The young married couple who had come to stay upstairs from us had had their first baby with all the usual aftermath of rejoicing and congratulations. A few days later my mother, as a 'very special treat', took me with her to see the new arrival. Before long she was fervently wishing she had not been so kind. As I took my turn to gaze upon the tiny morsel of humanity lying in his cot, someone rather unwisely said to me, 'Well, what do you think of him?' But I had a number of younger brothers and was quite blasé about babies, and replied quite unexcitedly, 'Babies look all the same, don't they?'

To put it mildly the new young mother was unimpressed by my reaction and my own mother, in the Motherwell colloquialism of our peers, was 'black affrontit'. When we were back in our own house, she lost no time in letting me know just how badly I had erred. I could not claim that I was never again to be guilty of putting my foot in it anywhere—far from it—but that episode probably reduced the number of times I did.

Before I drop the curtain on my early childhood reminiscences and the possible influence they may have exercised on my future work as a minister of the Church, let me tell you one thing more. My maternal grandfather was head gamekeeper on Barjarg estate in the parish of Keir in Dum-

friesshire and I used to spend every day of my school summer holidays there with my grandparents, going the day
after school went down and returning the day before it
resumed. There was one year that sticks out in my memory—I was seven at the time—when for some reason that I
do not recall no-one was able to escort me to my holiday
paradise. Nevertheless, there was never any question but
that Jim had to get to his beloved Barjarg as soon as possible,
and this he did by dint of careful planning and kindly co-
operation. It was, however, the kind of operation that would
be impossible to contemplate in our modern society with its
incidence of paedophilia and child abuse.

It was different then, vastly different. Those were days of
innocence, or so it seems in my recollection of them. Without doubt there was much more trust around and every
justification for it. My father put me on the train at Motherwell station with a request to a kind-looking lady in the
compartment to see that I was put off at Beattock. This she
duly did and I was met there by an aunt who worked nearby.
In due course, after tea and cake, she put me on the bus for
Dumfries where my grandmother was waiting to meet and
greet me and escort me to Barjarg.

It all worked with beautiful smoothness and I never
experienced the slightest anxiety along the way. The success
of the operation depended to a large extent, of course, on
being able to put trust in strangers to an extent that might be
highly dangerous today. This probably contributed to the
readiness I have had all my remembered life to take people at
their face value, a circumstance which contains both plus and
minus factors. It undoubtedly has rendered me more vulner-
able to deceit and betrayal but it has also, I believe, fitted me
better for the proper discharge of my tasks as a minister of
Jesus Christ.

Chapter Two

At Secondary School

WHEN AT THE AGE OF ELEVEN I proceeded to secondary education and became a pupil at Dalziel High School, it was somewhat accidental that I did, or, as I would prefer to describe it in retrospect, providential. I had proved to be quite a bright scholar and was Dux of my primary school, Dalziel Public. There were two non-denominational secondary schools in Motherwell, of which only Dalziel High offered the possibility of Higher Leaving Certificates and with them qualification for University entrance. Only those who attained a required standard in their final primary year qualifying examination—the 'Quali' of not very revered memory—were given the option of enrolling in Dalziel High.

It had a somewhat 'snobby' reputation in the minds of most of the predominantly 'working class' area of Motherwell in which we lived and it was only a comparatively rare bird who flew up from that environment to the lofty heights of Dalziel. It had never been discussed between my parents and me what my next educational step might be. It was simply assumed that I would be going on to Motherwell Central along with nearly everyone else. That, at least, is how I was regarding it when our teacher one day went round the class asking his pupils to indicate their preference. One after another, with a single exception, my classmates called out, 'Motherwell Central', and when my turn came, I went with the crowd and said the same. As the class dispersed, my teacher called me aside and asked me to invite my parents to come and see him. This they duly did and the upshot was that I went, after all, to Dalziel High.

My six years there were, on the whole, an extremely happy time, despite a rather inauspicious beginning when on my third day I was belted as a punishment for arriving late for afternoon school. I had slightly miscalculated the time, my home being a mile and a half from the school which made it a bit of rush there and back in the hour given for the lunchtime interval, and I reached the school just after the summonsing bell had ceased ringing. The gymnastics instructor, Sergeant Murdo MacKay, was waiting, as was his wont, to deal with latecomers. He proceeded to interrogate me in a brusque manner that struck terror into my young and very naive heart.

'Capitulate!' he thundered. For the life of me I could not imagine what he expected me to say or do in response to this command, so I stood motionless and dumb.

Again he thundered, more fiercely than before, 'Capitulate!' and once more I stood quaking and silent.

'No excuse,' he pronounced and led me off to his room where he administered two of the best on my outstretched palms.

It was some time later that I learned that what he was really saying to me was, 'What kept you late?'. But even if I had grasped that at the time, it would have made no difference to the outcome anyway.

Everyone, I am sure, has seen in his or her own life the truth of John Donne's oft-quoted aphorism that 'no man is an island'. Our lives are so inextricably interwoven and we owe so much—for good or ill—to the influence of others (as others do to us). One of the new friends I made at Dalziel in my first year class was William Dodd whose parents were also members of Manse Road Church. Because of Willie's invitation and appeal I enrolled in the Manse Road Boys' Brigade Company, 16th Motherwell, and that, in turn, had a

"Capitulate!"

lot to do with my hearing years later God's call to enter the ministry.

Our Boys' Brigade Captain, Tom Alexander, was an elder of the kirk and very keen to have 'his boys' attend morning church service as well as the mandatory B.B. Bible Class which preceded it. I was one of the large number of boys who yielded to his persuasions and so found myself Sunday by Sunday morning occupying a pew in the transcept of Manse Road Church along with other boys in the Company. The time came when I began to feel increasingly ill at ease during the service. As I listened to the minister in the pulpit—I was nearly sixteen by this time—another voice seemed to be saying to me more and more insistently, 'That is the job I want you to do.'

For a long time I resisted this, attempting to tell myself it was some kind of mental delusion. I trotted out to myself all sorts of reasons, many of them with seeming substance, for my not becoming a minister. Along with them I paraded before my mind all the much more appealing alternative careers I might choose. It was all to no avail. In the end I said, 'All right. If that's the way you want it, that's the way it'll have to be. But I warn you, I can't see myself being much good at it.' The very thought of standing up in a pulpit before a congregation was enough of itself to strike terror into my heart.

Nevertheless, once the decision was made, I felt an inner peace which left me in no doubt that I had made the right decision, indeed the only possible one. It was a very good thing that I was now convinced that it was God's call that I had heard, for the prospect of the ministry and its various ingredients remained unattractive and forbidding in my sight—preaching, visitation and the rest. This conviction of its being a call from God also helped to sustain me in face of the ribbing that inevitably ensued from some of my friends once it became known where I had decided to head.

My parents were extremely supportive once they learned of my decision although I have no doubt they were greatly disappointed to begin with. I suspect they had entertained other, more glamorous ambitions for their 'clever son'. They must have been dismayed, too, at the prospect of their eldest son going on to University for at least six years, earning no wage and needing support, when there were five younger ones to be fed and clothed. Nevertheless, they gave me every encouragement despite the sacrifice they must have seen it entailed for them.

To my lasting shame, I did not recognise this aspect of the matter at the time. I had yielded to God's insistent call that I should enter the ministry and that was that. To the ministry I must go. I bitterly regret not realising more than I did the measure of the sacrifice this involved on the part of my mother and father in those days before University grants— and that of my brother George, too, next in age to me. When my father was overtaken by the effects of his war wounds and died at the age of 46, in the same week as I graduated Master of Arts, George became the chief wage earner of the family and continued so until he himself went off to war and was killed in action in Germany in the closing days of the conflict.

At the time I was appreciative and grateful, make no mistake about that, but it was only in retrospect that I came to understand more fully how great was the sacrifice they were all so ready to make so that I might fulfil my destiny. That, I have come to see, is how it often is in life. Many a time we do not come to realise our indebtedness to other people until long afterwards—sometimes, sadly, only when it is too late to be able to express our thanks to them.

As I look back, I see that many experiences of my second-ary school period were eventually in their own way, some-times minor, sometimes major, to be of future grist to my ministerial mill. It was then, for example, that it came home to me in rather bizarre fashion that ministers, too, were human beings. When it became known that I was intending the ministry, Andrew Higgins, my own minister and a true Christian gentleman, took me out to lunch in order to discuss the matter with me. Naive as I undoubtedly was then, being not quite sixteen, when he suggested that I might wish to make use of the toilet facilities before sitting down to the meal, it was with a feeling of surprise and shock that I found him accompanying me. I do not suppose that I had any doubt that ministers performed the same bodily functions as the rest of us but it was only as he took up his stance beside me that day that it really came home to me that they did.

Andrew Higgins was not the only minister who invited me to have lunch with him once it was known that I hoped to enter the ministry. Rev. W. Wylie Fulton was the minister of Keir, the parish in which Barjarg lay, and which I attended when on holiday there with my grandparents, walking the three miles there and three miles back.

Mr Fulton was as delighted as Mr Higgins about my decision and had me along to his manse for lunch. I remember well his kindness that day but what I remember even more is having coffee at the end of the meal. I had never tasted coffee in my life until then. We were a tea drinking family and coffee was completely outside my range of knowledge. When the coffee was being served, Mr Fulton asked, 'Do you take it black?' Having no idea of the import of the question, I thought it polite to answer in the affirmative, nor did I have the sense to add sugar. I do not remember ever tasting anything which I found more unpleasant, not even the castor oil of earlier years, and I had considerable difficulty getting it over. I was wise enough to refuse a refill and it was a long, long time before I ever again ventured to drink a cup of coffee. Even yet, if I have to take it, I must have lots of cream and sugar.

In my late school days I entered into a brief dalliance with the local Baptist Church which carried over into my early University years. What attracted me was not the practice of Believer's Baptism but their strong evangelical emphasis. When I came to realise that such an emphasis was equally welcome in the Church of Scotland and that there was much more scope for it there, my dalliance came to an end but I remain grateful for the spiritual enrichment my Baptist sojourn afforded me.

I was, and am, equally grateful for the happy memories of my years at Dalziel High and not least for the memories of the friendships I enjoyed there. Some of these friendships, thank God, survive to this day, although others inevitably have withered with the passing of the years. There were some good friends, too, who did not survive World War Two which erupted the year after I went up from school to University. Just as sadly, one of my best friends, John Weir, did not even live long enough to meet the possibility of war service. A year or two older than I, he died of tuberculosis just as I finished my first University year.

Strange as it may sound, one of my deepest regrets concerning John is that he did not live to see me become a devotee of Grand Opera. He had long been an opera buff and tried many times to get me interested. Time after time he invited me to accompany him to one of the opera performances being staged in Glasgow, insisting that if only I would give it a trial, I would be sure to find it enjoyable. Time after time I declined his offer, convinced that the unpleasant caterwauling I then imagined opera to be was not for me.

The day did arrive when I became as much a lover of grand opera as John Weir had been but, to my sorrow, by that time John was dead. He would have been so pleased to know it and how I regretted not yielding to his pleas to give it a trial.

The basic trouble was that I was unaware of what I was missing. When I came to enter the ministry, I came also to realise that it is often for the same basic reason that many people turn their backs on the Gospel which all these years I have been seeking to proclaim. If only, my frequent thoughts have been, if only, as John Weir used to plead with me regarding the opera, if only they would give it a trial.

Chapter Three

The University Years

T HE YEARS I SPENT at Glasgow University saw me duly achieve the primary purpose of the exercise which was to graduate at the end of the first three year period with the degree of Master of Arts and at the close of the second triennium as Bachelor of Divinity (which latter I attained with Distinction in New Testament Language and Literature and with the Gold Medals in Hebrew and in Church History, a circumstance my proud mother would have wished me to mention, bless her). I was a conscientious student and absorbed a fair amount of learning during those academic years, a surprising amount of which has remained with me and some of which, perhaps even more surprisingly, has proved of considerable value in my ministry.

Even more useful for my future ministry was the manner in which these years induced a degree of maturity in the extremely raw schoolboy who first passed through the University gates at the age of seventeen and the manner in which they widened the horizons of a boy to whom even a visit to the city of Glasgow had previously been something akin to a very great adventure.

Not the least factor in my development process was the warm camaraderie I shared with the contingent of other Dalziel former pupils with whom I travelled by train back and forward to Glasgow. Each morning we packed into the same compartment of the 7.45 from Motherwell and, somewhat after the fashion of Tam O' Shanter, the morning invariably 'drave on wi' sangs and clatter', never much in the way of songs but always an abundance of clatter.

Here, too, lessons for my future ministry kept coming my way, unrecognised as such at the time but appreciated later. For instance, one morning a joke was told which had a mildly sexual connotation but which appealed greatly to my even then rather over-developed sense of humour. I burst out laughing and immediately one of my companions wagged a finger and said, 'Look at Jim Martin, laughing his head off at that joke and him going to be a minister.'

His reaction, albeit in kindly jest, indicated then what I found only too true in later years, namely that ministers are in a 'no win' position in that kind of situation. Laugh and you are too broadminded; refuse to laugh and you are too prudish.

They were a happy bunch of companions and I look back on those times of travelling together with much pleasure. And with much sadness, too. Two of that little band of fellow travellers—Robert Donaldson and Andrew Flockhart, both good friends of mine—did not live to complete their University course. Called to the colours, they lost their lives in action and the world was rendered a lot poorer as a result.

Not nearly as sophisticated as were some of my companions, I was one of the quieter members of that company and contributed little to the banter and the repartee. But there was one occasion when, I think, I did manage to light up briefly for the others a gloomy winter's day.

I almost missed the train that morning. Indeed, as I came racing down the stairs to the platform, the train was just beginning to pull away. There was no chance of reaching the compartment we always occupied in the middle of the train but I managed—just—to scramble aboard the very end one. I was poised ready when the train made its first stop, at Uddingston, jumped out quickly and raced full tilt along the platform until I reached the compartment occupied by my friends. Pulling open the door, I hoisted myself in, flung myself into the one vacant seat and gasped out, 'What a race that was. I thought I would never catch you up.' So sudden and so unexpected was my entry and so dramatic my little speech that for a couple of seconds of stunned silence, I think they really believed that somehow I had accomplished the extraordinary feat of keeping pace with the train all the way from Motherwell.

We were comrades in impecuniousness, too, although some of us were more impecunious than others. One consequence of this was that we normally walked all the way from Glasgow Central Station to the University, a distance of some three miles. The tram fare of three halfpence (old money, of course) was beyond our resources on a daily basis. If it was a particularly wet or snowy morning we might indulge in the extravagance of boarding a tram at Charing Cross which was roughly halfway, as this last, long stage cost only a halfpenny. More often than not, however, we walked all the way, whatever the weather, even though it might mean arriving for our first class thoroughly soaked and having to utilise the remaining minutes before the lecture commenced in entering the classroom early and attempting to dry ourselves out a little by pressing up against the old-fashioned, wide-diametered radiators which encircled the walls.

The homeward journeys of that first University year also linger vividly in my memory. We all had different courses and this meant that only Barclay Miller and I travelled home together. This we did on the 1.45 pm train and on the journey we used often—childishly, perhaps, and certainly agonisingly—to talk about food, for the simple reason that the subject was much in our minds. After a hurried, scanty breakfast around 7.15, neither of us had eaten anything since, so that here we were, six and a half hours later, heading for home and the lunch that was waiting for us there. Given the circumstances it is not surprising that we should have tortured ourselves so often as we did by thinking and speaking of delectable dishes (of food).

"attempting to dry ourselves out a little"

It was during my University years that my father died. As already mentioned, it was the same week as I graduated M.A. This added poignancy to what was a very sad occasion for all of us. At the time I was most conscious, I confess, of the poignancy I myself was feeling. It was only later—and even more now as I look back over the years—that I came to ask myself how poignantly sad it must have been for my mother to be a witness in the selfsame week to the funeral of her husband and the graduation of her eldest son.

It was during my University years that there came into being two of the great loves of my life—for Marion Greig who in course of time became my wife and for Grand Opera. I mention them together because the latter development was not unconnected with the former and because each of them, in a way, came about as a result of my making response to a call to serve.

In the grim days of war, blackouts and the rest, Manse Road Church bravely decided to launch a new venture and found a Life Boy Team. My very good friend, Jimmy Johnstone, agreed to be Leader-in-Charge and when he invited me to be one of his assistants, I felt it my duty to accept. Soon afterwards he said to me, and well I remember it, 'That's it all set up now. We're going to make a beginning next week and I've arranged with a young lassie from the church who is a very good pianist to come and play for us. Her name is Marion Greig.' A few years later, as was to be quoted by the Rev. James Currie at my Welcome Social to High Carntyne, 'Jim Martin married the girl who played the piano at the Life Boys'. And so my decision to give what help I could with the Life Boys in Manse Road Church turned out to be a very fortunate one for me—again 'providential' is probably the more correct adjective.

Less directly it led also to my conversion to Grand Opera. One day in 1942, John MacKelvie, one of my friends in the Faculty of Divinity, suggested to me that I should take Marion to an opera performance. The Carl Rosa Company were about to present a season in the Theatre Royal,

Glasgow and he felt that what he was proposing was sure to further my standing as a suitor with Marion since unlike me she was a musician.

I was an absolute philistine in fact so far as music was concerned and the prospect of a night at the opera was in itself no more appealing to me then than when John Weir had vainly tried to woo me in its direction. I was, however, allured by the prospect of at one and the same time pleasing Marion and enhancing our courtship. John MacKelvie suggested 'Rigoletto' as a good opera to attend and so I booked seats for that, reconciling myself to an evening of musical boredom or worse but counting the sacrifice worthwhile.

In the event I was confounded and transformed. To my surprise and relief I found the opening scene tolerably pleasant although I could not help wondering how I would feel after three hours of the same. But the next scene made me opera's willing slave for evermore and elevated me to heights of such ecstasy as I had never imagined possible in such a context.

Gwen Catley was singing the coloratura soprano part of Gilda, the ill-fated heroine of Verdi's opera, and when she began the aria 'Caro Nome', that was the beginning of my operatic captivity! I was enslaved from that moment on and still am. The irony of it is that my passion for the opera has never been fully shared by Marion for whose sake I went to see Rigoletto in the first place. There must surely be some kind of parable in this.

Like every divinity student who has ever been, in tandem with my academic studies I served some sort of preaching apprenticeship during my time at University, doing pulpit supply here, there and almost everywhere. So far as numbers were concerned I assuredly did not start at the top. My very first preaching engagement saw me with a congregation of three, in Taynuilt Baptist Church, but that was at the morning service. By evening word of my preaching must have got round for there was an increase in attendance of no less than $66^{2}/_{3}\%$, the congregation having risen to five.

Joking apart, it was rather a chastening experience. I was so sure that I had been called of God to preach the Gospel; I had worked hard in the preparation of my services; I had travelled a long way in order to proclaim my message; and the numbers assembled to 'sit at my feet' were only three and five. It was a great disappointment.

At the same time, as I well recognise now, that experience was of no little value for the future. For one thing, it reaffirmed very strongly for me Jesus' declaration that where two or three are gathered in his name, he is there, too. For another it brought me face to face in the most challenging fashion with the responsibility (and privilege) of the preacher to give of his best whatever the circumstances and whatever the size of his audience. I believe that that initiatory preaching experience was a factor in my being able to claim as I look back now over the delivery of thousands of sermons, that I have always tried to be mindful of the individual hearer whether I was looking from the pulpit at that original three or the eight or nine hundred who Sunday by Sunday for many years formed my regular congregation at High Carntyne.

My student supply preaching was instrumental, too, in highlighting for me the foolishness as well as the discourtesy of unpunctuality. I was to conduct the services in a church in Clydebank and turned up on the Sunday morning well in advance of the eleven o'clock starting time. This was my usual practice in order to acquaint myself with the surroundings and the normal procedure; but I need not have been quite so early. Having done all my preliminary reconnaissance work, I was left to cool my heels in the vestry until twelve minutes past eleven before the church officer came to pilot me to the pulpit.

'Have I made a mistake?' I enquired. 'Does the service start at 11.15, not 11?'

'Oh, no' was the reply. 'It's supposed to be eleven but we never start then because the bulk of the congregation never come until after the hour.'

It struck me very forcibly at that moment that so long as the service started late, so long would the bulk of the congregation continue to turn up late, too. In consequence of that experience, all through my ministry I was determined that every meeting and every service over which I had control would start, if at all possible, precisely at the scheduled time.

It was in the course of one of my long distance student preaching expeditions that I was given a rather discomfiting illustration of the danger of a euphemism being misunderstood. Because of the distant location of the church I was to supply, I required to have weekend hospitality. As was common practice in those days, this was given me in the home of members of the congregation, two elderly sisters. They were most hospitable but, although they showed me my bedroom and gave me a splendid supper, they did not say anything at all about toilet facilities.

The result was that as the evening wore on, I became increasingly uncomfortable. At last I was compelled to seek relief.

'May I wash my hands, please?' I enquired somewhat diffidently.

'Certainly' the sisters chorused in unison, and brought me a basin of hot water, towel and soap.

Chapter Four

Locum At Newarthill

THE NEXT STAGE IN MY APPRENTICESHIP for the ministry was the eighteen months I spent as locum tenens in Newarthill Parish Church, some two miles distant from my Motherwell home. The war was still raging in Europe and the Far East and the minister of Newarthill, Alestair Bennet, was away serving as an Army Chaplain. This was long before the days of the Probationary Year, obligatory training now for nearly every student on the completion of his divinity course. Men—and it was only men in those days—might go straight from college to their first charge or, more likely, they might serve as an assistant or a locum for a longer or shorter period.

I was invited to be assistant to the Rev. R. G. McConnochie in the West Parish Church, Airdrie, and was on the point of accepting the invitation when something intervened. Rev. James Ritchie, of Motherwell's Brandon Church, who was interim-moderator of Newarthill during Alestair Bennet's absence, asked me to be locum tenens there. It seemed a more attractive proposition. It involved much less travelling—I had, of course, no car—and it would bring me more much needed money. I was to receive £200 a year which in the hard up state of self and family was quite a lot. Perhaps just as attractive was the fact that in Newarthill, unlike Airdrie, I would have a pretty free hand.

Whether or not I personally and my future ministry would have been the better of the discipline of an assistantship can never be known. I rather suspect it might. But I thoroughly enjoyed the year and a half of my locumship in Newarthill and I have no doubt that my experience there was of enormous benefit to me in my future work.

During this time I was performing, as best I could, all the ministerial functions except those requiring an ordained minister, that is, baptisms, marriages, communions, presiding at kirk session meetings. In other words I was having a lot of the job satisfaction of the ministry with very little of its job frustration. Unlike a minister in a charge, I did not carry the ultimate responsibility. Quite the reverse. The congregation were exceedingly grateful for anything worthwhile I succeeded in accomplishing, and exceedingly tolerant of anything less than successful. What they saw with generous eyes was a very young and very raw learner who was kindly trying to lend a helping hand in their minister's enforced absence.

Things went very happily indeed for me in that eighteen months, and with a lot of apparent success as well. At any rate the two services of worship I conducted there each Sunday were well attended and so was the Bible Class/Youth Fellowship I ran for the young people. This is not to suggest that everything was smooth sailing. There was, for instance, the occasion of my first Remembrance Sunday service. Our Professor of Practical Training had advised us students that the Benediction ought always to be the closing act of any and every service of worship and that if, for instance, the national anthem was to be sung, it should be before the benediction, not after it.

As Remembrance Day approached, I discussed the form of service with the elders. When I explained that I intended to have the national anthem before the final blessing, one of the elders, who also happened to be the local councillor, offered violent opposition. He appeared to regard this arrangement, particularly since the country was at war, as almost treasonable and said so in no uncertain terms. The others, fortunately, were more accommodating of my view and were helped towards that end, perhaps, by the fact that I was very willing to conduct the traditional short remembrance service beside the village war memorial. From that sticky sort of beginning, whenever the national anthem has been sung in a service that I have been conducting, it has been sung prior to the benediction being pronounced. My old professor would have approved.

Criticism of that sort, however, was rare and for the most part my temporary ministry in Newarthill went swimmingly so far as I was concerned, a circumstance which is the usual lot of those engaged on a ministerial locum tenens. Even yet, over a gap of many years, I recall many features of my time in Newarthill with a warm glow of mingled joy and gratitude.

There was the carol singing at Christmas round the village. Both Christmasses I shared with the folks of Newarthill saw me join with them in that. We gathered at the church—a mixed and somewhat motley crew of all ages— and from that starting point we made, on two successive nights, a sweep of the entire village, following a carefully planned itinerary and taking up about three hours each night. I had never been involved in that kind of open air carol singing before and for me the first one was a specially marvellous experience. The particular circumstances no doubt contributed to the impression made on me. The ground was frostbound and the stars shone ever so brightly from a clear sky. The street lights were severely dimmed to conform with blackout regulations, as were the torches we carried both to help us see our way and also to read the words on our carol sheets.

I hope that our singing those two Christmasses that were the last one of the war and the first one of the peace, conveyed something of the eternal glad tidings of the season into the Newarthill homes that heard us in those long past but never to be forgotten days of austerity and anxiety. We certainly got a lot of fun out of doing it, even when we found ourselves left in the dark. It was the Christmas after the war ended. The street lights were back to full volume and we did not need to carry torches. But we had forgotten that these were still austerity days and that the street lights all went off at a certain time; either that or our timing had gone awry. In any event we were still in full voice at our last stopping place when suddenly the lights snapped off; and we had to creep back slowly and carefully in convoy to the church hall and the cup of tea awaiting us there.

The blackout added romantic quality to our carol singing expeditions but it could well have meant the finish of me one night, aided, I confess, by my own stupidity. Buses, too, were permitted only a very subdued form of lighting both inside and out. This, combined with the similarly restricted street lighting, meant that alighting from a bus could be a hazardous affair unless great care was taken. It was imperative to wait until the bus was completely at rest before stepping off since it was virtually impossible to see either road or pavement while standing on the platform. For the same reason it was often quite difficult to determine whether or not the bus had yet come to a total stop. One night, thinking that the bus had come to a standstill, I stepped blithely off and immediately began to turn a series of involuntary cartwheels which ought at the very least to have resulted in broken bones. By some freak of fortune, or gift of providence, I suffered no more than some extensive bruising to my body which was as nothing compared with the severe bruising to my pride, aggravated by the concern of the conductress and passengers who crowded out of the bus to see if I was still alive. (The very next week a man, under the impression that his now stationary train had drawn up at the Motherwell station, stepped out. In fact the train for some reason had been halted some distance short of the platform. He fell to the track and was killed.)

I was always ultra careful from then on, I assure you, whenever I had occasion to disembark from bus or train in the blackout.

That was one incidental lesson that I learned during my

"I stepped blithely off"

Newarthill sojourn. There were others. One was my introduction to Burns' Suppers. I had never previously been to such a function but it was, as it still is, an annual highlight of Newarthill's very active Church Club. Burns' Suppers can be, as I have since discovered, of varying quality and while some may be most enjoyable, others can be very tedious. The Newarthill one came into the former category.

My horizons were widened further during my year and a half at Newarthill by my being invited to conduct a short fortnightly lunchtime service in the British National Electric factory (BNE) which was located at the Carfin end of Newarthill. Someone in the works had started up a twenty minute service for the employees every second Wednesday lunch break in a large hut adjacent to the canteen. It was already well established before I happened along and there were no less than thirty present when I took my first service there.

I would not claim that I was anything like spellbinding. I was raw and gauche in a great many respects. But I was sincere and I was enthusiastic. And I stuck rigidly to the time allotted me. I had to, or I would have found myself holding the platform in an empty hut. When the factory whistle blew at the end of my twenty minutes, my congregation simply could not wait a moment longer. They had to go to work on the instant. Fortunately I never failed to finish before the whistle. Perhaps it was because of this more than anything else that the numbers swelled. By the time I had to take my farewell on being called to Newmilns, the Wednesday attendance had risen to nearly a hundred—as much, I believe, a sign of the days of war in which we were living as of anything else.

At the conclusion of my final service I was completely nonplussed when there was not the usual speedy evacuation of the hut-cum-chapel in anticipation of the restart whistle. As I looked around in some bewilderment, the works manager ascended my little platform and proceeded to shower me with kind words and generous gifts on behalf of my 'congregation'.

The hut which formed our little church has long passed from the scene and the factory itself has long since ceased to be; but even yet I never drive along the road beside which they once stood without thanking God for the tremendous privilege it was to be allowed, callow youth that I was, to minister to such a body of men and women clearly hungering for a word from the Lord in time of crisis. I only hope that now and again I may have succeeded in speaking the word that someone wanted or needed to hear.

Newarthill has always been (and always will be) associated in my mind with certain memories of an unusual character. Such as the time when I had dressed up for the Bible Class Hallowe'en party in a manner that was more grotesque than aesthetic without taking into consideration how I was to make the two mile journey between my home and the village hall where the party was to take place. This was long before the days when I possessed a car, nor did I know anyone who could give me a lift. The alternatives were that I should walk or that I should take the bus. The physical feat of walking presented no problem: I frequently walked to and from the church. The problem was the inquisitive, perhaps even suspicious, stares I was sure to be subjected to even in the restricted visibility of the blackout. Taking the bus presented the problem of being exposed to the somewhat brighter illumination of the bus interior. Since the latter was going to mean a much shorter period of exposure than the former, I took the bus. I did get a few stares and a few chuckles but I was heartened by some cheery words from the conductress who, after enquiring what was afoot congratulated me on my courage. Her congratulations were completely undeserved as I was inwardly quaking but they helped me to ignore one lad in the bus who remarked to his companion in a loud whisper which I was obviously meant to hear, 'Ah wonder if his mammy knows he's oot.'

Equally vivid in my memory is the way that Mrs Buchanan insisted on my having a bath in her house after playing in a football match nearby for the Bible Class. Her son, Wilson, was one of the stalwarts of the team and when his mother learned that our next match was to take place on the pitch very close to their house, she told him that I was on no account to be allowed to go home unwashed like the rest, but was to come over to the house for a hot bath. I was embarrassed at being offered such privileged treatment and protested that I would really prefer to be just 'one of the boys'. Mrs Buchanan would have none of it. It was unthinkable that the young minister should not have a post-match bath when the house was so near.

As it transpired, it was a wet night and a muddy pitch and as I lay soaking in the warm water afterwards, I refused to allow my pleasure in it to be spoiled by thinking too much of my less fortunate team mates wending their mud-bespattered way home or of Wilson who was being kept out of his bath by my occupancy of it.

What was almost my final service as locum in Newarthill had also a rather bizarre twist to it. The day before, playing football for Dalziel F.P.s against Whitehill at Craigend in Glasgow, a ground I was to come to know very well when I went to High Carntyne, I sustained a broken toe which ended up in plaster. Despite having considerable difficulty in making my way home, it did not enter my thick head that I was likely to have the same difficulty, or worse, in making my way to Newarthill the following morning. Came the morning, however, and I found that walking was almost impossible. How I was going to get myself round to the main road and the bus stop was a nightmare prospect. I had severe doubts as to whether or not I could make it and having no telephone made my plight even worse.

Then salvation arrived at the door in the person of my college friend, Jim Aitchison. Not being himself engaged that Sunday, he had decided to come along on his motor bike and worship under me before I came to the end of my time in Newarthill. Since he was in good time, he had called in to offer me a lift on his pillion.

It was like manna from heaven. Certainly it was deliverance from my predicament. I very much doubt if I could have got to Newarthill Church that day without Jim's unexpected assistance. As it was, although in considerable pain and difficulty, I managed to scramble astride the pillion seat of his bike and so got transported to Newarthill. Once at the church, I contrived to hoist myself into the pulpit and take up position there for the service. After that Jim took me home again.

A memory of a different kind that will for ever be associated in my mind with my time in Newarthill is of my brother, George, being killed in action in Germany. Serving with the 2nd Battalion of the Cameronians for some eighteen months, he had been with them in the horror and the carnage of the Anzio Beachhead, and in the subsequent breakout and push to Rome. After that had come a rest period in Palestine before the battalion was drafted to Germany to add its weight to the final drive for victory in Europe. In Germany it was in action only once, when George's company ran into an ambush in the little village of Bleckede on the River Elbe. It was the 21st April 1945 and nineteen of the company lost their lives, including my brother.

It was the month of May before news of his death reached us. Final victory in Europe was clearly imminent and this was much in my mind as I prepared for the Sunday services. It was just then, with the victory bells all poised to ring throughout the land, that a letter came with the morning post to my mother announcing baldly that Rifleman George K. Martin had been killed in action in North-West Europe. He was 21 years of age and VE Day was just at hand.

Forty five years later when I came to speak at a Holy Week service in Newarthill, a member of the congregation recalled how the hearts of the congregation had bled for me, for my mother and for my brothers as I led their worship on that Sunday which followed our receipt of the news. That was a measure of the warm, loving fellowship with which the people of Newarthill Parish Church embraced me and which is such a happy memory for me still.

Chapter Five

My First Charge

W HEN I RECEIVED THE INVITATION to preach as sole
nominee for the vacant charge of Newmilns West
in the Irvine Valley, I did so, oddly enough, with
more than a twinge of regret. Like all my contemporary
divinity students, I had been making application for vacant
churches and was keen to get fixed up with a congregation
and parish of my own. In the fashion of the time—things are
somewhat different nowadays—we paid little or no attention to the larger congregations. It was generally accepted
that a man should seek a congregation of a small or moder-
ate-sized membership for his first charge before venturing to
tackle anything larger.

I had applied not only for the vacancy at Newmilns but
also for a vacancy in Strathaven; and was particularly hoping
that the Strathaven one would be successful. This was for no
more spiritual reason, I fancy, than its greater proximity to
my home town of Motherwell. Since I was a person who had
travelled afield very little, Strathaven had some small measure of familiarity to me while Newmilns was totally
unknown. What was no doubt even more important, my
fiancee lived in Motherwell and since we were not planning
to be married until the following year, that made Strathaven
even more attractive because of its nearness to Motherwell.

What happened was that both vacancy committees came
to 'hear' me in Newarthill and both appeared to be reason-
ably impressed. My hopes ran high regarding Strathaven and

rose even higher when, a week later, the interim-moderator informed me that I was likely to be chosen as sole nominee at the committee meeting shortly to take place. The very next morning I received a letter from Newmilns asking if I would be agreeable to preach there on a leet of four, two chosen by the Vacancy Committee and two nominated by the Transference of Ministers Committee in Edinburgh as the regulations required. I wrote back indicating my willingness to do so, elated that I was going, so it seemed, to have the best of both vacancy worlds. Newmilns would not be making their decision until more than a month hence by which time my Strathaven hopes would have been either realised or dashed.

Three days later I received a telegram from the interim-moderator of Newmilns West Church which ran: 'Invite you to be sole nominee. Letter following.' Next morning the promised letter informed me that the other candidate selected by the committee had declined to preach on a leet. The committee had decided, therefore, to abandon their interest in him and invite me to be sole nominee, the necessity to hear two Edinburgh nominees no longer pertaining.

This was undoubtedly good news but it had its disappointing side, too. My delight was severely tempered by the thought that I was likely to be asked to go to Strathaven where my heart at that moment lay. If only Newmilns had been pursuing their original procedure!

Knowing that the meeting of the Strathaven committee was imminent, it was only right that I inform them without delay of this new development. I made my way to the nearest telephone kiosk and informed the interim-moderator that I was no longer a candidate, having just been invited to be sole nominee at Newmilns.

'I am very sorry to hear that,' he replied, 'as I have just this morning put a letter in the post inviting you to be sole nominee for the vacancy in Strathaven. The committee made their decision last night.'

I was sorely tempted to accept the Strathaven invitation

but I knew that I would never be able to live with my conscience if I did. If I were to hold to my belief that a call to minister to any particular charge ought to be a call from God, then surely the invitation that came to me first had to be taken as God's wish for me. That, at any rate, was how I saw it; and that was how I decided. And so it was to Newmilns West that I went as minister of my first charge. Was I unduly naive in my way of thinking then? Perhaps I was, but although I have sometimes wondered, I have never really regretted my decision.

The date was soon fixed for me to preach in Newmilns as sole nominee. It was arranged that I would travel from Motherwell by bus on the Saturday evening to be met at the bus stop by one of the elders, Matt Anderson, who would escort me to the home of another member of the congregation, Miss Maggie Miller, who would give me overnight accommodation. As it transpired, she had to give me some first aid treatment as well.

Although at that time I was playing football on Saturday afternoons for Dalziel High Former Pupils, it did not occur to me that it might be prudent not to risk injury by playing the day before such an important engagement, especially since I would require to board the bus for Newmilns almost immediately after the match. In any case my football career up to then had been remarkably free from any injury of note and I had no reason to think that it would be any different on this particular Saturday afternoon.

Nothing serious did overtake me that day but it was the start of a run of misfortune which also took in the receiving of my call at the Presbytery of Irvine and Kilmarnock, my first wedding and my first baptism. On the Saturday in question nothing very much happened to me except that I took a heavy tumble on the earth pitch which was our home ground and sustained some quite severe gravel rash on my right arm. The post-match shower cleaned it, however, and I felt none the worse.

I encountered no problems in making my way to Newmilns. I alighted at the correct stop. Matt Anderson was there to meet me. Miss Miller made me very welcome. Excited though I was at the approaching 'ordeal', I slept well; but in the morning I did not feel so good. My arm was swollen and inflamed; and before she would permit me to go off to conduct the morning service, Miss Miller insisted on bathing and bandaging it. Whether or not this had any effect either for better or for worse on my 'performance' that day, I cannot tell. However, after conducting the evening service, too, I was duly elected to be minister of the congregation and parish of Newmilns West Church. This was on the 23rd of February 1946.

The next stage was the presentation of the call by the congregation to the Presbytery for its approval. This was done on Tuesday, March 5th. It was on the intervening Saturday that I suffered the broken toe injury referred to in the previous chapter. In consequence, when the call was sustained at the Presbytery and I was invited forward to have it placed in my hands, I made my way to the front with a very pronounced limp and with the aid of a walking stick. This had an amusing sequel. Many years later I encountered a minister who that same day as I received my call was taking leave of the Presbytery to go to a new charge.

He had not set eyes on me since that day and when we met, he exclaimed in obvious surprise, 'I see you are walking normally now. When did you get it put right?'

'Get what put right?' was my puzzled response.

'Your lameness' he replied, 'When I last saw you, you had a bad limp and walked with a stick.'

When I explained about my football injury, he confessed somewhat apologetically that he had been quite convinced that I was the victim of some kind of accident or congenital deformity that left me with a permanently lame leg.

My broken toe prevented me playing again before I was ordained and inducted on April 11th; but I was fit to play the following Tuesday night which happened to be the eve of my first marriage ceremony. In this match I somehow

"Miss Miller insisted on bathing and bandaging it"

contrived to get myself kicked on the face in attempting to head a goal. The result was that on the day of my first ever wedding I was sporting a many-hued 'black eye' with lacerations to accompany it. I did not then normally wear my spectacles out of doors but I was forced to put them on for the wedding as some measure of camouflage for my damaged features. How effective was the attempted camouflage is a matter of some conjecture but no comment was passed.

By a strange coincidence I was again the victim of a facial injury immediately prior to my first baptismal service. Playing my first game for Kello Rovers—at Auchinleck against the local Talbot—I sustained a cut above the eye which necessitated some stitching by the local doctor. Over the stitches he affixed a rather prominent dressing and that was how I was forced to present myself to the congregation and perform the baptism the next day—no camouflage possible on this occasion. The stitches were removed by my own Newmilns doctor on the Tuesday and on the Wednesday morning I met Mrs Browning on the street, the oldest member of the congregation and the lady who had 'robed' me on my induction night. Observing my eye now free from its dressing, she said to me in genuinely sympathetic tones, 'I'm so pleased, son, to see that your boil is better."

Football may seem to have occupied an inordinate amount of my time but it was not in my opinion wasted time, not all of it anyway. Not only did it help my general physical fitness and so, I believe, contribute considerably to my being physically more able for the multifarious tasks of the ministry, it also enabled me to get alongside many men in the parish to an extent that would not otherwise have been likely. And many of the boys, too.

I used to take our Life Boys team regularly to the public football park for a football session. Since the Newmilns public park was then at the very top of the high hill surmounting the town, even beyond the cemetery, the mile or so walk uphill was a good bit of exercise in itself before we had even begun to kick a ball around; and what a lot of fun, not least for me, those Life Boy games provided.

So did our Youth Fellowship matches, although they were much more serious affairs. We played against the other Youth Fellowships in the Irvine Valley and, although always sporting, the matches were played with a fierce determination to win. This determination led to one rather unfortunate accident. For one home game, against our chief rivals from the neighbouring town of Galston, we found ourselves a man short when we assembled at the pitch. Rather than start at a numerical disadvantage, and with the concurrence of the opposing team, I prevailed on the father of one of our players to make up the number. Jimmy McColl played very well and enjoyed himself to boot, until an awkward fall caused him to dislocate a shoulder and rendered him unfit for work for a couple of weeks. I felt really bad about that but at the same time was delighted that with Jimmy's help we had notched up a victory.

In addition to the Youth Fellowship 'friendly' matches I was playing competitive football all the time I was at Newmilns. After two markedly undistinguished seasons with Kello Rovers and Kilmarnock Juniors respectively, I returned to my first love, Dalziel Former Pupils. My most vivid football memory from my time in Newmilns is, however, rooted in none of these but is of the year when at long last Motherwell won the Scottish Cup.

They had come very close to achieving this success and had been defeated finalists no fewer than four times during my period of following their fortunes. The first was when I was a very small boy, too young for my father to allow me to accompany him to Hampden Park in Glasgow where Motherwell's opponents in their first ever appearance in the Cup Final were the redoubtable Glasgow Celtic who had won the trophy on more occasions than any other club.

This was well before the advent of television and even radios were not the possession of many. We certainly did not have one nor did any of my friends. Our local newsagent, however, arranged to keep in touch by telephone with the ground and relay the score as the match progressed by displaying a notice prominently in his shop window.

I for one was already in a state of high excitement that crisp April day by the time my father went off to get the special train that was taking supporters to the match. I could scarcely contain myself as the hands of the clock crept round ever so slowly towards the kick off time of three o'clock. At last three o'clock came and by then I had already joined the band of eager hopefuls who had gathered on the pavement outside the shop window, boys of similar age to myself, a handful of men who for one reason or another had not been able to make the journey to Hampden, and a surprising number of women.

Once more the time seemed to pass with agonising slowness until the shop assistant emerged to fix a notice to the window. I pressed forward with the rest in an agony of suspense and in a moment a great sigh rose in unison heavenward, whether of relief or disappointment I cannot say, as we read: Fifteen minutes played: Motherwell 0, Celtic 0. But the next appearance of the assistant provoked a spontaneous howl of delight, 'Motherwell 1, Celtic 0'. Suddenly the sun was brighter and the day warmer. Before long we were delirious with joy as the notice was changed to read, 'Motherwell 2, Celtic 0'. As the second half proceeded and the score remained unchanged I was enraptured. Surely my heroes could not fail me now—and there was an additional bonus for me personally if they won the cup. A neighbour friend who took a great interest in me had promised to buy me a pair of football boots, my very first, if they did. What a day this was going to be.

When the notice in the window read, 'Fifteen minutes to play: Motherwell 2, Celtic 0' the day became brighter still and the sun even warmer. Then came what seemed the happiest moment of my young life. A notice was placed in the window which read, 'Final score: Motherwell 2, Celtic

1'. Now I was in ecstasy. The Cup was ours—and the football boots were mine.

Then, disaster. Before we had dispersed, still shouting and cheering, the shop assistant was seen to emerge again, take down the notice and replace it with another. Thunderstruck we read, 'Corrected result: Motherwell 2, Celtic 2'—I can see it still so clearly in my mind's eye, blue-pencilled on white paper. In the dying seconds of the match, when hundreds of Motherwell fans were already on their way home to celebrate their team's triumph, Allan Craig, the Motherwell centre-half, had accidentally headed an aimless crossball into his own net.

Suddenly the sun had disappeared and the air had turned chill. I was heartbroken and on the verge of tears. As I shuffled homewards, head bent low, my neighbour friend met me, 'I'm so sorry about the result' she said ever so kindly, 'But I'm going to give you the boots just the same.'

'I'm not caring about the boots,' I whispered in my misery, 'We've lost the Cup.'

And so we had. Celtic won the replay by four goals to two.

Two years later Motherwell again won their way to the Final. Again Celtic were their opponents and again Motherwell lost, this time by one goal to nil. My only meagre consolation was that once more I was spared witnessing the defeat, being still reckoned too young to be risked in a Cup Final crowd.

In 1939 Motherwell reached the Final yet again. By now I had entered University and was able to attend the match in person accompanied by a crowd of my old school friends. How confident we all were. Motherwell were playing so well and this time we did not have our bogey team to face. Clyde, our opponents, would surely be swept aside, and I would be there to see it. Clyde refused to play their expected part and had the temerity to win 4-0.

In 1951, now the minister of Newmilns West, I found myself once again making the journey to Hampden Park in high expectation that at last Motherwell were going to win the Scottish Cup. Admittedly our adversaries were the mighty Celtic, so often our downfall in the past, but surely it must be our turn this time.

My confidence in the outcome was such that I prepared my children's address for the next morning on the assumption that by then Motherwell F.C. would be the proud holders of the trophy. I borrowed one of the spare first team jerseys when at Fir Park for my weekly training session the week of the match, planning to show off its claret-and-amber loveliness to the congregation, to speak of wearing the colours of one's side and so to speak of wearing the colours of Jesus Christ.

Almost unbelievably, so far as we Motherwell supporters were concerned, it was another defeat. Of course, as always, Motherwell were desperately unlucky, and there was the usual crop of 'if onlys'; but the stern fact remained that the score which went into the record books and determined the destiny of the cup that year was, 'Celtic 1, Motherwell 0'.

At church service on the Sunday morning I still made use of the football jersey, perhaps I was too numb (or dumb?) to think of anything else. It was not, however, the gladly exuberant occasion I had anticipated although I did speak about the victory that was sure to follow donning the colours of Jesus.

When Motherwell made their way into the final for a second year in succession, I went off to Hampden to see them play Dundee with much less optimism than the previous year and, indeed, with a pronounced feeling of foreboding, a feeling shared by my companion of the day, my friend and fellow Motherwell-sufferer, Jimmy Johnstone. Imagine our delight when after a goal-less first half our team took command to win by four goals to nothing.

The memory of what follows remains as fresh in my memory as the game itself. It began with the official Motherwell party, self included, making its joyful way to Motherwell in two special buses and then making a slow, triumphal procession through the streets of the town and its environs. This was followed by a celebratory meal in a local restaurant, in the course of which Allan Craig, the unlucky centre-half of 1931, leaned across to me and said through tears, 'I've waited a long time for this but I'll sleep better from now on.' Over-sentimental, over-dramatic, exaggerating a mere football match to a ridiculous extent? Of course, but I fully understood how he felt and was in accord with his feelings.

The official celebration was followed by another, unofficial one in Tom Cumming's cafe close to the ground where most of us were in the habit of dropping in for a cup of tea after training. There the match was played over and over again into the small hours, with all the analyses and conjectures being neatly put into place by John Aitkenhead of the magic left foot when he commented, 'When we've exhausted all the "ifs" and "buts", the morning papers will still say, "Motherwell 4, Dundee 0" and that's all that matters.'

In case I may have given the wrong impression, let me plead that, despite my undoubted passion for it, the game of football was only a small part of my ministerial life in Newmilns. There were many more important things occupying my time and my attention, chiefly the ministry of word and sacraments to which I had been called and for which I had been ordained. This involved the church services of worship with their component parts of preaching, praying and the rest, the visiting of my parishioners in hospital and in their homes, the conducting of baptisms, marriages and funerals, the presiding over a host of meetings, the addressing of many more, and so on and so on.

It all may sound very serious and so it was because, as I understood it, I was in a real sense attempting to minister to that congregation of Newmilns West 'in Christ's stead'. Very serious indeed because very important, but not necessarily dull and solemn and not always so. I recall many lighthearted moments and experiences from those Newmilns times, some of which may be safely recounted without risk of offence.

I did not immediately occupy the manse on my induction. The fact of the matter was that Marion and I did not have enough money to furnish the manse sufficiently for us to take up residence in it and we planned to be married in June of the following year. For the intervening period of a year and a bit I was given accommodation as a paying guest in the house where I had lodged overnight when I preached as sole nominee. This was an admirable arrangement for me, and Miss Miller proved to be very kind.

One kindness she did me was to send me to take driving lessons so that I could on occasion drive her car. I was most reluctant to accede to this suggestion of hers since there was no immediate prospect of my acquiring a car and in fact I did not do so until I had left Newmilns. But she was insistent and I finally yielded and in due course passed my driving test.

Maggie Miller's own driving was virtually a legend in the town, and deservedly so. She must have been, I am almost convinced, the archetypal character of the (chauvinistic) story of the lady driver who, arriving at the back of the queue awaiting admission to heaven, was instantly ushered by St Peter to the head of the line and through the gates. When the world-famous evangelist standing at the head of the queue protested at this seeming unjustifiable favouritism, St Peter answered, 'Well, you see, despite all your many wonderful sermons, the fact is that her driving has struck the fear of hell into far more people than your preaching ever did.'

Miss Miller learned to drive fairly late in life and always crouched fiercely over the steering wheel which she held in a vice-like grip. One disturbing consequence of this was that whenever she was engaging in conversation with a passenger in the front seat or, worse, in the back seat, she was inclined to turn towards the passenger and turn the wheel at the same time, causing the car to make all sorts of frightening changes of direction which paid not the slightest regard to other traffic.

A devout Christian and faithful church member, Miss Miller had very firm, very conservative and very unyielding views about the rights and wrongs of many things to do with the church; and was never slow to give expression to them. One of these had to do with the proper ministerial garb for a funeral. When my first funeral came along and I was about to leave the house to conduct it, outwardly calm—I think— but inwardly quaking with apprehension, Miss Miller stopped me in the hallway.

In tones which might well be described as 'aghast', she said, 'You're not going to a funeral like that, I hope.'

As neat and tidy as I could make myself and wearing my dark Sunday suit as I was, I was much taken aback, 'Why, what's wrong?' I asked in trepidation.

'Where's your hat?' she thundered.

I never wore a hat in those days and did not even possess one. When I told her this, Miss Miller became even more aghast.

'Every minister I have known' she pronounced in tones of utter condemnation, 'including your two colleagues in the town, has always worn a tile hat to a funeral. To do anything else is to show great disrespect.'

I tried to protest that, as I saw it, not to wear a tile hat to a funeral was no mark of disrespect to the deceased nor was going bareheaded. She would have none of it and refused to allow me out of the door until a compromise was reached. She brought out her deceased father's tile hat which, in good condition, she had stored away. It did not fit me but I agreed to carry it with me to the funeral, even though it could not be worn, and that seemed to satisfy the requirements in her eyes. As I left, nevertheless, I could hear her muttering to herself, 'No dignity, no dignity.'

A day or two later, to my great embarrassment, she presented me with a beautiful tile hat. I was appreciative of her kindness because I realised how strongly she felt on the matter but I was appalled at her attempting to coerce me into what she reckoned the proper mode of conduct despite being aware that I did not share her view. Not only so, the thought of me, who had never worn headgear of any sort since my school cap days, stepping it out along the main street of Newmilns with this 'lum hat' on my head, splendid example of the genre though it was, filled me with horror.

In the end another compromise was made. For my next two or three funerals I carried the hat with me although I never put it on my head. This seemed to satisfy all the requirements of decorum and respectfulness so far as Miss Muller was concerned for no word of disapproval was uttered. After that I stopped even taking it with me and, to my surprise and relief, it was never again mentioned.

Miss Miller's concern for me and the proper discharge of my ministerial responsibilities continued even after I married and no longer lived under her roof as, for instance, in connection with the lighthearted revue 'November Nonsense' I produced along with my Youth Fellowship members. I had started up a Youth Fellowship in Newmilns West in addition to the already existing Bible Class and this inevitably took up a good deal of my time. In the second year of the Fellowship's existence, by which time it had become strong and vibrant, we decided to embark upon a 'show'.

Since I was the producer, as well as one of the cast, this took up a great deal more of my time. Miss Miller did not view my enthusiasm for the Youth Fellowship and for November Nonsense with delight. Rather the reverse if the truth be told; and one day she said to me, almost with a sniff, 'You'll need to watch the amount of time you spend with the young people. Don't forget it's the older people who pay your stipend.'

Nevertheless, I pressed on and, fortunately, not only did the Youth Fellowship continue to thrive and play a significant part in the life and work of the congregation but November Nonsense also was a great success. We had hired the Morton Hall, the largest capacity building in the town, for two nights, Friday and Saturday, and managed to sell all 900 seats. The capacity audiences gave us a tremendous ovation which did not encourage our humility one little bit. On the Saturday morning I was still quite intoxicated by the heady wine of the previous night's applause and found this topped up by a flood of congratulatory remarks as I made my usual walk through the town for the morning paper. It was a good job that I was well aware that I was near perfect and therefore immune to the temptation to become conceited about it all.

Seriously speaking, the main feature of the exercise was that it was good for the young people involved, despite the gloomy forebodings of Miss Miller and some others. They enjoyed it and it unmistakably enriched the spirit of camaraderie which already existed in the group. It was very much a team effort although, as with most team efforts, some individuals stood out. Willie McColl was one of these. Endowed with great natural comic talent, he was the centrepiece of much of the comedy in what was essentially a music and laughter show. Imagine, then, the consternation of producer and cast when Willie was unable to appear at the dress rehearsal owing to an attack of the asthma which had afflicted him from childhood. The message received from his home assured us that if at all possible he would be present at the performance the next night but warned us that this would be out of the question unless there was a marked improvement in his condition.

Since we had no understudies for any of his parts—who ever heard of a church production like this having understudies?—I was in a real spot of bother. We endeavoured to cover Willie's various parts as best we could at the rehearsal but since most of us were already playing a number of parts, this was far from easy, and no one could be expected, especially at such short notice, to match the quality of performance we were expecting from Willie. To everyone's intense relief Willie did appear for the first performance, although clearly much under the weather. Despite being poorly he was the star of the show and was even better on the Saturday by which time he was considerably improved in health.

Maggie Miller was only one of many 'characters' who added rich colour to the scenario that was Newmilns West Church during my ministry there. Ernest Ling was another. A Londoner, he had come to Scotland and adopted the Church of Scotland as well as the Irvine Valley in his youth. Ordained to the eldership at what was then the unusually early age of 29, he was already long and firmly established as session clerk by the time I came on the scene. A man of intensely evangelical fervour, he was extremely anxious to ensure as far as possible that everyone else, particularly his minister, should adhere to the correct line (that is, his line) theologically. This occasioned him, as I have recounted in *It's You, Minister*, calling on me frequently on a Monday morning to chide me sadly when there had been any straying from the right path in the previous day's preaching.

It may well have been out of similar concern for my behavioural rectitude that on the first New Year's Day after our marriage he called at the manse door at seven o'clock in the morning. Ostensibly his mission was to present us with a calendar and to offer us his good wishes for the ensuing twelve months; but I could not help wondering, because of what seemed the unearthliness of the hour, if he was just anxious to make sure that the minister was sober and in possession of all his faculties. I passed muster on these accounts but I was somewhat befogged by lack of sleep, having not got to bed until four o'clock after bringing in the New Year in the neighbouring manse of Loudoun Old with our good friends the Hewitts. Had Mr Ling somehow got wind of our going there?

Ernest Ling was a most zealous Christian. This, in the main, was a source of pleasure and encouragement to me as his minister; but it could and did lead to some disconcerting moments, too. Like the time when, a year or two into my ministry, the minimum stipend was raised to £410, having been £370 when I was inducted.

"He called at the manse door at 7 o'clock in the morning"

Ernest came to see me in an obvious state of excitement. He came to the point without delay.

'I felt I had to have a word with you about the new stipend level.'

'Oh, yes' I replied encouragingly, expecting a word of congratulation that the stipend level had reached such a notable milestone; but there was a surprise in store.

'I regard it as a matter for regret and concern' he said in sepulchral tones. 'Now that the minimum stipend has topped £400, I fear that the ministry may become a job instead of a calling. Men will be tempted by the fleshpots being held out.'

'Fleshpots' was, I assure you, the word he used. He was patently sincere in his concern but I did not share his opinion that £410 a year, with no expense allowance, was likely to lure anyone into the ministry as a materially comfortable way of life, not even in 1948. I could not help regarding it as a bit incongruous that such an opinion should be expressed by a man who was the owner and managing director of a hosiery factory and who drove a large car whose annual running costs would exceed my stipend.

Willie Nimmo was a character of a different type. Not affluent in worldly goods, he had a pawky sense of humour. It scintillated when he was fit and well; and even when he fell victim to an illness that was to prove terminal, its light did not grow dim. When I called upon him then, as I did frequently, he always had a smile and never failed to have a quip of one kind or another, combining it all with a wonderfully steadfast faith. I will never forget one visit in particular, shortly before the end as it turned out.

'How are things going?' I enquired.

Weak and ill though he was, he mustered a smile and whispered, 'With the help of God and a store loaf, I'll pull through yet.'

And then he added, 'Whatever happens, I'll pull through anyway, you know that.'

Mrs Mathie, too, was a character. She kept a little news-

agent-cum-confectioner's shop and was a very faithful
attender at church. She was never absent from her pew—
except on the Sunday of the local Fair Holiday. This was the
time when practically everyone in Kilmarnock and district,
including the Irvine Valley, was on holiday. A great many
went away from home for the holiday. Mrs Mathie never did
but on that particular Sunday she never came to church
either. I could never work out the reason behind the rigidity
of her observance of that holiday Sunday abstention from
church.

A characteristic of many Newmilns people, paralleled in
most small towns, was an excessive interest in and knowledge of other people's business. For 'incomers' like us,
accustomed to the greater anonymity of a large town or city,
this could at times prove irksome. We were not used to being
constantly exposed to scrutiny like goldfish in a bowl and it
was difficult at times not to get ruffled, even though the
inquisitiveness was nearly always of a kindly nature.

We soon learned to live with it and so I did not find it
anything other than mildly amusing the day I visited old Mrs
Macfarlane who lived on the main street underneath the
manse which was perched on a hill overlooking the town.

'You were a bit later than usual in getting up this morning, I noticed' she remarked.

'As a matter of fact we were' I said in some surprise,
'How did you know?'

'Oh' she answered matter-of-factly,' I look right up at
your chimney from my window and I usually see the smoke
start to rise at seven o'clock. This morning it was getting on
for eight.'

There were occasions when the Newmilns knowledge of
other people's affairs was far from being accurate. On one
memorable occasion this placed me in a situation of great
potential embarrassment. I had been visiting Willie
Hamilton on a regular basis for some time because he was a
very sick man. One day when I called he was noticeably
much better than he had been for some time and I went away

uplifted and full of hope. The next morning I was walking along the main street of the town when one of our members hailed me.

Sad of face he said, 'Pity about Willie Hamilton, isn't it?'

'What do you mean?' I asked in dismay, 'He was a lot better when I saw him yesterday. Don't tell me he's taken a turn for the worse.'

'Oh, I thought you would have heard. He died this morning.'

'That's a terrible shock' I replied, 'He was in such good form yesterday, I'll just go along now and see his wife.'

Which is just what I did. Fortunately for me, when she answered the door, Mrs Hamilton spoke first.

'Hello,' she said brightly, 'I didn't expect to see you back again today but you're very welcome of course.'

Deducing correctly from her tone that Willie's passing, like Mark Twain's, had been somewhat exaggerated, I mumbled some near incoherent nonsense about being in the vicinity and taking the notion to pop in and see Willie again who was, as a matter of fact, even better than he had been the day before. I am sure my explanation was totally unconvincing and that after my departure Mrs Hamilton would spend a little time puzzling as to what had brought me back again so soon. But how much worse it would have been if I had got in first at the door with some such remark as, 'I'm so sorry to learn of Willie's death and I've come to offer my sympathy and help.'

The richest vein of memory deriving from my time in Newmilns is, not surprisingly, that which is rooted in my own family life. These were the years that saw my marriage and the birth of our two daughters.

With my marriage I left my 'digs' in Miss Miller's house and took up residence in the manse. Grateful as I was to Maggie Miller for much kindness, a year had been quite enough to be so close to her watchful eye. Anxious to mother me, she was often in danger of smothering me. As a married man, occupying the manse, life acquired a new and richer dimension.

Marion, for her part, in addition to everything else found herself saddled with the Presidency of our Woman's Guild. The tradition still persisted at that time in most churches that where there was a minister's wife she ought, *ipso facto*, to be the Guild President. When I arrived the office was held by Miss Flora Mackenzie, the local postmistress and a formidable lady, as well as an efficient one. We were only a few days returned from our honeymoon when Miss Mackenzie 'waited upon' the minister's wife.

Following an exchange of pleasantries, she got right down to business. She never saw any point in beating about any bushes. 'You'll be taking over the Presidency of the Guild, Mrs Martin'—a statement rather than a question.

'Oh, I've never been a Woman's Guild member and never even been to a Woman's Guild meeting, except once when I played the piano accompaniment for the soloist. I'll be very pleased for you to carry on as President for my first year anyway.'

But Miss Mackenzie's mind was firmly made up.

'That's out of the question,' she rasped, 'It's the job of the minister's wife. It always has been like that and I'm stepping down now.'

That, as it turned out, was that. Neither Marion nor I was sufficiently experienced—or brave?—to do anything other than accept the position as Miss Mackenzie declared it had to be. And so it was that my very young and very shy wife began a career of what eventually amounted to twenty-six years of Woman's Guild Presidency. This was made up of all the rest of our time in Newmilns and nineteen of the thirty-four years spent at High Carntyne, including a spell there of sixteen consecutive years before, to her relief and joy, the Guild adopted a constitution limiting tenure of office to three years at a stretch.

I take my hat off to the way she managed to do it and do it so well, despite having at the same time to look after a home and a family and a husband who was so foolishly workaholic that he did not spend nearly so much time with his wife and family as he ought to have done. For my part, nevertheless, many of my happiest Newmilns memories revolve round my family life.

Not a few of the funnier ones, too. There was, for instance, the time when our elder daughter, Heather, at the age of two, extensively decorated her sleeping father's face with raspberry jam. She had been left in my care after our evening meal while her mother attended to some other chores before completing the clearing of the table. Obviously exhausted by another hard day's work, Heather's father dozed off in his armchair. This circumstance, combined with the fact that one of the items left on the table was a jam dish, led to my being abruptly wakened some time later by the sound of uncontrollable laughter pealing forth from my dear wife's mouth as she entered the room to see me sound asleep and my features covered in the raspberry jam which Heather had, no doubt lovingly if not artistically, smeared all over them.

It would have been embarrassing for me if any of my congregation had chanced to call at that precise moment and caught sight of my jam-decorated face. It would have been even more embarrassing for me on another occasion if I had not succeeded just in time in composing those same features into serious mien before processing with my fellow Presbyters into church for the first induction service to take place after my own. There was I, the most recent ordinand amongst the ministers and therefore the first of them to enter the church (juniores priores) and as we were being lined up prior to entry, Willie Marshall, minister of Reid Memorial, Hurlford, nudged me and said, 'Do you see that elder over there, do you know who it is?'

'I do not' I replied.

'Well, that's David Lammie, session-clerk of Easton Memorial, and a fine man. He is a well-known draper in the town.'

Then Willie went on to say with a solemnity in keeping with the seriousness of the occasion, and with the cherubic countenance I came to know as his trademark but which then left me quite unprepared for what was coming, 'His shop had a sale last week. There was a notice in the window which read: Don't miss this. Lammie's trousers are down again.'

I wanted to explode but at that precise moment we received the command to begin the procession. It was torture as I marched into church to my first induction service as a presbyter all the while fighting desperately to suppress the peals of laughter which were clamouring inside me to be allowed out. Willie Marshall meanwhile was sauntering in with the same beatific expression that was his constant companion.

I found it a bit of an ordeal to control the hilarity Willie's comment threatened to produce in me but it was a different kind of ordeal I underwent when our first child was born. Everyone knows how much expectant fathers go through; anyone of them will tell you, although conceding graciously that expectant mothers have a bit to suffer as well.

Heather was born after a night of electrical storms which sent thunder rolling through the Irvine Valley for long periods and lightning flashing round our manse in spectacular fashion. I had arranged with Jim Dykes, the local taxi driver, that we would call him whenever the time came for Marion to be transported to Kilmarnock Maternity Hospital. That time arrived at six in the morning and a beautiful morning it was now that the storm had passed.

Jim was swift to respond to my call and soon Marion was being received in at the hospital by a very efficient and, to my mind, surprisingly unexcited sister—was she not aware that my wife was about to have a baby?

'That's fine, Mr Martin' she said brightly, 'There's no need to wait. Phone in about ten o'clock and see if we have any news for you. And don't worry. We're delivering babies here every day, you know.'

All very well for her to talk, I reflected, as I was driven back home. They were not delivering *our* baby every day.

Lesley chose to come while I was conducting Sunday morning service. This time our good friend, Jim Wylie, one of our church elders, had offered his services as chauffeur to Kilmarnock Maternity. The summons came most inconveniently around seven o'clock on a Sunday morning. Unborn babies clearly have not been trained as they should to consider the convenience of their parents. After Jim had taken us to Kilmarnock it was a case of hotfooting it back to Newmilns and of my making a hurried and somewhat distracted finalising of my preparation for the morning service.

As it happened a vacancy committee—from Carstairs—chose that very Sunday to come and run the rule over me as a possible new minister for their church. To see and hear me at my best, or even at my normal, they should probably have chosen some other Sunday. At any rate they did not pursue their interest any further.

It was, then, in the manse of Newmilns West Church that Marion and I began our married life together and our two children spent their earliest days. It was a splendidly built house and magnificently situated high above the town, at the top of a steep flight of steps known locally as Jacob's Ladder. It was, however, extremely difficult and expensive to heat. Few manses had central heating at that time and few financial courts gave any thought to an allowance for heating and lighting.

There was no such luxury as rising on a winter's morning to an already heated house or even of switching on some instant heat. Instead, it was a matter of forcing oneself out of the warm bed, hurriedly throwing on some clothes and starting on the necessary chore of raking out the dead fire of the previous night, removing the ashes, setting a new fire and finally getting it going for a new day. Our two main rooms had huge fireplaces which were voracious devourers of coal. They shed considerable heat into the room but just as much up the wide chimney; and draughts of icy air seemed to invade the rooms from all sides. The end result of all the expenditure of time, energy, temper and money was that we were invariably roasting hot at the front and freezing cold at the back.

Heather did not seem to feel the cold at all that Christmas morning when, at the age of three, she made her way unsuspected downstairs at some unearthly hour to open the presents Santa Claus had left at the foot of the Christmas tree and, particularly, to take possession of the tricycle which had been her chief wish from Santa. Marion and I had gone to bed almost as excited as Heather, this being her first Christmas with a real awareness of Santa Claus and all that entailed.

We were looking forward with great anticipation to the thrill of seeing her face when she saw what Santa had brought. When we woke at six, we were surprised that she had not yet come through to wake us and be taken downstairs to see if Santa had been. Then we heard a sound from below and when we investigated, there was Heather astride her tricycle and riding it in triumph round the room. All the other presents had been unwrapped and examined and she had clearly been on the go for quite some time. And so, after all, we missed the precious moment we had been so looking forward to, and all because we failed to take into account the possibility of our little daughter making her way to the Christmas tree without first coming to us. It shows that we ought never to underestimate the capabilities of others, especially children, to do the unexpected.

Memories of our years in Newmilns crowd in upon me as I write. Some, as might be expected, stand out because they were 'firsts' for me—first baptism, first wedding, first this, first that. One was when for the first time ever I worked at my desk all through the night. I had never done this before, even as a student, but one Friday night in the month of June I was faced with little alternative if I was to be properly prepared for my two Sunday services.

It had been an exceptionally busy week for me and I had

been able to do little or nothing towards making ready for Sunday; and Saturday was already heavily committed, culminating in the evening with the Golden Wedding celebration of a couple in the congregation, another first for me. Circumstances therefore decreed that I must finish my preparation for Sunday before thinking of going to bed that Friday night. In the event I was still working at it when dawn broke and what a gorgeous dawn it was. It made all the hard slog of the night before well worthwhile. The sun came up 'trailing clouds of glory' and its coming was accompanied by a bird chorus of almost indescribable beauty. My weariness was tossed aside like a blanket and my heart sang with the sheer joy of being alive on such a morning.

The exhilaration produced in me by the rare privilege of greeting the dawn and its handmaidens on a morning like that helped me greatly to get through the day without feeling unduly tempted to sneak off into some quiet corner and fall asleep, even by the evening when I was presiding at Mr and Mrs McGhee's Golden Wedding.

That experience illustrated what surprising feats can be accomplished when the adrenalin is flowing freely. There was one other night in Newmilns when I worked at my desk all night and the adrenalin undoubtedly took command. One evening after supper I decided to start writing a paper I was to deliver to the Men's Club the following week. It was to be on the evidences for the truth of the Resurrection of Jesus and as I worked on it, the subject gripped me and I found myself writing on and on, reluctant to break off what was becoming an increasingly fascinating task. I did not stop until the paper was completed and by then the new day had come. It was a most satisfactory night's work for me not only because it set me up for my Men's Club assignment but also because the paper written on that overnight shift later became the nucleus of my first ever book, *Did Jesus Rise From The Dead?*

Not all my most vivid Newmilns memories are particularly church-orientated. One of a more secular character was an adventurous journey into Glasgow in order to see and hear the great Swedish tenor, Jussi Bjorling. He had been my favourite singer ever since Sid Barker of my New-arthill Bible Class introduced me to his voice at a gram-ophone record session in Sid's house. Now had come an opportunity to hear him in person. He was to give a concert in Glasgow's St Andrew's Hall and three of my young friends were also keen to attend—Willie McColl, Adam Martin and Willie Wright. I obtained four tickets and arrangements were made to drive in in Adam's car.

It was the middle of winter and on the day of the concert the weather was severe. Road conditions were appalling with ice, snow and fog. The descent of darkness added to the hazards. No sensible person would have attempted the jour-ney in such circumstances. But we were not of a mind to be sensible that night. We were determined to make our ren-dezvous with Jussi Bjorling, realising that we would in all probability never have another opportunity to see him; and so, after a hurried council of war by telephone, we decided to venture.

Although Adam drove with extreme care, the twenty mile journey was positively hair-raising, one of many slithers and slides and of necessity very slow. Although we had left in what seemed ample time, we arrived at St Andrew's Hall, relieved and out of breath, on the stroke of the concert's starting time. We knew that it was a sell-out but the hall was less than half full when we entered; and we had barely taken our seats when there was an announcement to the effect that, owing to the fog and the bad driving conditions, the concert would begin thirty minutes late to allow the large number known still to be on their way to have that period of grace.

The journey back did not seem half so terrifying as the inward journey had been but, of course, we no longer had any anxiety about the time and, what is more, we had had our feast of song. Bjorling had been every bit as good as we had expected him to be.

That was an instance of pleasure mingling with anxiety.

The mixture is not all that uncommon but much more common in every minister's experience is the mingling of joy and sorrow. So often, for instance, in my High Carntyne days I would find myself leaving a funeral service to head straight for the church and a marriage ceremony.

One of my most vivid memories of a day in which the joyful and the heartbreaking were part of the same afternoon is of Newmilns and January 31st 1953. Early in the afternoon of that day I conducted the marriage of two of our young people. It was a very wild and stormy day but the weather cast no chill over the wedding proceedings. The wedding itself went off smoothly and after it we repaired to the local Co-operative Hall for the reception. This, too, was a happy affair with the guests politely laughing uproariously at the minister's jokes.

Then in the middle of it all we heard of the sinking of the Princess Victoria. That was a black, black day in Scottish maritime history. The M.V. Princess Victoria, en route from Stranraer to Larne, foundered in the Irish Sea with heavy loss of life, and some of the lost were known to some of us in that so happy wedding party. Never was the fragility and transcience of human life borne in upon me more dramatically.

That fragility and transcience confronted me every time I conducted a funeral service. While my Newmilns funerals were only a small fraction numerically of the many hundreds I was later to conduct in Carntyne, each one told that same message in its one way. In my Newmilns period cremations were a rare occasion for me and in all my seven-and-a-half years there, I conducted only two cremation services. All the rest of my funerals were burials and nearly all of these in Newmilns Cemetery high on the hill above the town.

Nevertheless, one of the most vividly remembered was to Tarbolton. It was the only one in my ministry which had to be postponed because of weather conditions. During March 1947 I was still lodging with Miss Miller and usually spent a day off each week in Motherwell. One Wednesday afternoon I went to Hampden Park to see the Scottish League play the English League in what was at that time an annual encounter, accompanied by Charlie Robertson, an inside forward of note who was then playing for Motherwell. The match was played in bitterly cold conditions and as it finished flakes of snow began to fall. After a quick snack, Charlie and I went our separate ways, with me going out to Motherwell to spend the night at home, never imagining that so late in March the snow might present any problem on the following morning. But it did with a vengeance. I woke to find that it was lying feet deep and near panic assailed me. What if the buses were off? What about the funeral I was scheduled to conduct in Newmilns at two o'clock that afternoon? Would I manage to get there?

Once up and dressed I learned that the buses *were* off and that roads all over the country were impassable, including that between Motherwell and Newmilns. Panic redoubled until I discovered that it was possible to reach Newmilns by train via Glasgow. What a relief it was finally to take my seat in the Newmilns train at Glasgow. Although it was running considerably late as it huffed and puffed its way through the snow-covered landscape, I knew I was going to be in plenty of time to walk home from the station and change for the funeral. It was just as well that I had time in hand because when I left the sheltered confines of the station it was to find myself struggling through snow that was chest-high in places.

Progress through such deep snow was slow and exhausting and I was greatly relieved to stumble at last through Miss Miller's door, aware that I would have time to snatch a bite to eat as well as change before I needed to venture out again. But I had more time for that bite than I was expecting. A telephone call from the undertaker informed me that the road to Tarbolton was closed and that there was simply no way the funeral could take place that day.

'Will it be tomorrow?' I enquired.

'I don't know' was the reply, 'It depends on the weather.

We'll just have to play it by ear and have it the first day that the road is open enough to let us through. At the moment it looks as if we might have to wait a week.'

To his surprise and to the relief of all concerned, the funeral was able to go ahead the next day. The intense cold continued but there was no further snow and superhuman efforts cleared the road sufficiently for it to be passable with care. The funeral went off without mishap but I shall always remember the snow piled high above the car roofs on either side of that road to Tarbolton.

Miss Miller, ever concerned that I should not only do the right thing but clearly be seen to be doing the right thing, was inclined to be critical of my spending the night in Motherwell—day off or no day off—when there was threat of snow. But it was, after all, the middle of March and the snow falling at the end of the football match was very slight. In any event, as we discovered later that day, the bus I would have caught if I had decided to head directly for Newmilns ended up stuck deep in a snowdrift, perhaps with ironic appropriateness at the village of Moscow on the Volga. Some of my young people who had also been at the match were on that bus. Finding shelter overnight at a nearby farm steading, they had to walk all the way home in the morning before making their way, very belatedly, to work.

Chapter Six

From Country Town To City Parish

M Y SECOND CHARGE WAS UTTERLY DIFFERENT in many ways from my first, as different as was the manner of my appointment to it. This time it was not the end result of an application from me to be considered for it. This time the invitation to be sole nominee came completely unsought. In consequence I was all the more convinced that it was the calling of God that I should go to High Carntyne. That conviction never deserted me and this has proved a source of much comfort in times of stress and strain.

So far as I was concerned, it began with a telephone call to me from William Barclay. He informed me that he had recommended me to the vacancy committee of High Carntyne who proposed to come and hear me the following Sunday if I was willing that they should. This came as a bit of a shock. I had never heard of High Carntyne and had to confess that I did not even know where Carntyne was. Willie Barclay assured me that there was a real job to be done there, that he felt I was the man for the job and that he hoped I would give it serious consideration.

The next Sunday morning the vacancy committee duly descended upon Newmilns and the West Church, all twenty-five of them. There could be no secrecy about such a large contingent of strangers adding itself to my 150 strong congregation that Sunday morning, all the more so since they arrived by special bus and went in before the service to

Kate McGhee's Tea Room, which was the eyes and ears of the town. After the service I met with the committee, all of them, in the Session Room, and for half an hour they asked me a lot of questions, and I asked a few of them. All that time Marion was waiting anxiously in the manse, wondering if soon she would be leaving it, our first home together. That, however, was a question I was not yet able to answer. The committee had appeared to be favourably impressed but that, I realised, might have been no more than politeness.

The question was answered the following Wednesday evening. At that time Marion and I were in process of entertaining the kirk session several at a time to an evening in the manse and one such group was with us that very evening when I received a phone call. It was from Rev. John McPhail, minister of St Andrew's East in Glasgow who was the interim-moderator at High Carntyne. He informed me that the vacancy committee had that same night decided unanimously to invite me to be their sole nominee. Would I accept? Thrilled and excited though I was, I told him that I would need to see High Carntyne and also to talk the matter over with my wife before making a final decision.

Next day Marion and I took the bus to Glasgow where John McPhail met us and drove us round the parish, before taking us to the church where we sat in the vestry and talked with him for a spell about the congregation. It was a depressing sort of day, gloomy and drizzly, and it had a depressing sort of effect upon us. Neither felt at that moment particularly exhilarated about the prospect of leaving the country to live and work in this part of the city of Glasgow; but all along I had had the strong conviction that, coming as it did completely unsought, the invitation from High Carntyne must be a call from God. There was, therefore, never any real doubt but that we would say 'yes'—despite the dismal forebodings and warnings of some friends and acquaintances about going to a church with such a heavy work load and such a heavy burden of debt as it then had.

I preached as sole nominee and was duly elected. On

January 17th 1954 I conducted my final service in Newmilns West. That same week I was inducted to my new charge where I remained until my retirement 34 years later. We moved into the High Carntyne manse on the Monday, I was inducted on the Wednesday, there was a Welcome Social on the Friday and on the Sunday morning I was 'preached in' by the same William Barclay, later to be Professor of New Testament Language and Literature at Glasgow University and a household name for his writing and his broadcasting. My abiding recollection is that heavy rain greeted us for our entry into the manse and that it seemed to rain heavily with little or no interruption for the next six weeks.

I certainly have very clear memory of the downpour that accompanied the service of induction and of how the torrential rain of that evening was paralleled by the torrential rain of the evening of the induction social. Despite the weather, my ministry was given a heartwarming send off by the presence of some six or seven hundred people on either night, including two busloads from Newmilns. Since my birthday is January 21st, I was able to say with literal truth to the congregation at the welcome social on January 22nd that being their minister had already 'put years on me'. This lighthearted remark was in its way somewhat prophetic of the 34 years ministry that lay ahead.

My first Sunday on my own in the High Carntyne pulpit afforded a pointed illustration of how even in church circles human relationships can sometimes be tricky. Robert McCrae Brown, our session clerk, informed me that he was to have a meeting with the church choir after the morning service, to hear a complaint about the slight they reckoned they had been dealt by the kirk session bringing in solo singers from outside to provide the musical entertainment at my welcome social. Some of them, he told me, were highly indignant and he anticipated having a difficult time.

It so happened that for my children's address that morning I used the old fable about the man who along with his son was taking a donkey to the market. The message was that it is impossible to please everybody at the same time and we ought therefore to try simply to do what we see to be right. The service over, Bob Brown went off to fulfil his assignation with the choir and I wished him well. To my surprise he was back in the vestry in less than five minutes.

'Has the meeting been postponed?' I asked.

'Oh, no, that's it over,' he replied with a smile.

'How did you manage to get through it so quickly?'

'I just said to them, "You heard the minister's children's address this morning. Well, that's how it was so far as the kirk session's action is concerned. Nothing more needs to be said." '

It scarcely struck me as the most diplomatic manner in which to handle what was clearly a delicate situation; but I soon discovered this kind of direct approach was typical of Bob Brown. He was very down to earth and his speech was always brief, sometimes to the risk of being brusque. He never seemed to suffer any anxiety afterwards about how he had handled any particular situation or about anything he may have said. I often think now—ruefully—that I might have been much the better of taking a leaf or two out of this particular book. My desire generally was to seek the most tactful solution possible for any given problem and to avoid upsetting anyone unnecessarily; but, as I discovered to my cost at times, this approach on occasion had the result of permitting someone or other so large a say that the hoped for injury-free solution was put further out of reach.

Robert McCrae Brown was a great support to me but his seeming passion for brevity was in danger sometimes of sending me up the proverbial wall. Some churches have suffered from kirk session minutes that were too verbose; Bob Brown's were so terse as frequently to offer little or no information to the posterity that might in later years come to read them. When, for instance, a year after my coming to High Carntyne, I was reading through past minutes for the purpose of writing a booklet to mark the semi-jubilee of the congregation, I came across the following entry in Bob's handwriting: 'The kirk session considered the problem with the Girl Guides.' The next month's record stated: 'The kirk session dealt with the problem in the Girl Guides.' Not very informative and not very helpful to any would-be historian who might have considered the subject one worth chronicling.

This was a style he never changed. He was such a good friend and such a good church-man that I hesitated to run any risk of causing him offence but I did venture once or twice to suggest that a fuller minute might sometimes be in order. It was to no avail. There was the time, for instance, when I myself had put forward a suggestion for a new congregational activity. His minute read: 'The kirk session discussed Mr Martin's suggested new activity.'

'Mr Brown' I protested mildly, 'That gives no indication of what the suggestion is.'

'No' he admitted, 'but it's not necessary to say any more. Everyone knows what it is.'

'Perhaps so' I replied, 'but who will be able tell from that minute in fifty years time what it is.'

'In fifty years time' he said with a laugh, 'It won't matter one bit whether anyone knows or not.'

So I gave up and we continued happily in the same rather cryptic fashion of kirk session minuting. One indisputable advantage was that the minutes never took very long to read through.

No ministry can ever be completely static and my High Carntyne years were full of vigorous congregational activity, sometimes intense activity, especially when, as was frequently the case, we were making innovations or attempting experiments.

Most of the time the kirk session was very supportive of whatever fresh agency the minister might be introducing to further the gospel cause—but not all of them all of the time. My recommended introduction of the Young Worshippers' League was one that aroused fierce opposition on the part of one elder.

It was a disappointment to me to discover when I began my ministry in Carntyne that very few children came to the church service on a Sunday morning, although the Sunday School was numerically strong and well attended. Accordingly I set about trying to encourage the young people to attend worship and I thought it might help if we began the Young Worshippers' League which many churches had for that very purpose, enrolling children between 7 and 14 years and awarding book prizes at the end of each session to those who had attended well. When I put this up to the kirk session, Frank leaped to his feet in high dudgeon.

'Do we want the peace and solemnity of our worship disturbed by the noise young children are bound to make? It will be time enough for them to come to church when they are old enough to understand all that's going on and to be able to sit quietly without being a nuisance to the older people.'

His attitude was, of course, totally in opposition to mine and fortunately proved to be very much the minority view. A number of other elders pointed to Jesus' own welcoming attitude to children. Frank, however, was not finished.

'Even if it's a good thing to encourage children to attend church, and I don't agree that it is, bribing them to come with the offer of prizes is surely an unworthy way to do it.'

Nevertheless, overwhelming approval was given and the Young Worshippers' League soon became an integral part of the High Carntyne scene. I used to think to myself whimsically in later years that if I were to suggest dropping it, voices would be raised in protest that this had *always* been part of our church and that it would be monstrous to change it.

Changing an established pattern has generally been a hazardous enterprise in most congregations. A story is told of a beadle of the old school who lay dying. The position of beadle which he had held for forty years was now to pass to his son and the son said to him, 'Father, have you any advice to give me regarding my church work?'

'Aye,' said the old man, 'Resist a' improvements.'

That sadly has too often been the way of it. My effecting a change in our Harvest Thanksgiving celebration was a case in point. High Carntyne had for long what might be termed a traditional type of Harvest Festival—with the congregation bringing to the church on the Saturday gifts of fruit, vegetables and the like. The Woman's Guild committee arranged these into a colourful display for the Sunday services, and after the evening service the same ladies made them up into parcels for distribution round the sick, elderly and housebound in the parish, the names and addresses being supplied by the minister.

There was much to commend this method of celebration—the attractiveness of the church display, the opportunity to express one's gratitude for God's providence, the taking of gifts to some poor souls in need of uplift. After a few years, however, it became only too evident that there was another side to the picture. There was a large element of waste in the operation. Many of the recipients, although mostly grateful to be remembered, neither needed nor desired a harvest gift (although human nature being what it is I once received an anonymous letter complaining that the parcel received had been inferior to that of a neighbour 'who doesn't attend church so regularly as I do'). The surplus of fruit and vegetables which we sent to local hospitals more often than not involved waste, too, since they proved an embarrassment of riches at a time when other churches were engaged in a similar operation. There was also considerable waste of time and energy on the part of the Guild ladies who had to labour usually until after eleven o'clock on the Sunday night to wrap up in excess of 300 parcels.

I suggested, therefore, to the kirk session that we change our harvest procedure. The idea was that we would arrange a token display of harvest produce but invite the congregation to bring a gift of money to be passed on to Christian Aid. Agreement was almost unanimous and the change was made with considerable benefit year by year to people in need in

the third world. Most people voted the change a great success and with only minor alterations that was how we celebrated our harvest thanksgiving all the rest of my High
Carntyne ministry. Yet almost to the end an occasional voice
would be heard complaining, 'I really liked it better the way
it used to be done.'

Sometimes I met with opposition which in a paradoxical
kind of way was created by approval of what I was achieving. I am a firm believer in the value of the parish system,
certainly in a situation such as ours where we were the only
place of worship within our parish boundaries. In line with
this belief I was keen on the kind of parish mission where
every now and again all the houses in the parish received a
visit in a spirit of friendship and invitation from members of
the congregation going out in pairs.

It so happened that following my induction church attendances rose dramatically until we were frequently having to
bring in extra seats on a Sunday morning to supplement the
850 which comprised our normal seating. When, after a
couple of years, I proposed that we have a Parish Mission,
Alec Kincaid, always a loyal supporter of me and my work,
jumped to his feet in protest.

'That would be a foolish thing to do' he cried. 'What's the
point in inviting more people to come to church when we
have difficulty in seating the ones we have now?'

All attempts to persuade him that this was the sort of
problem any church would be delighted to have completely
failed to impress him. Although the mission went ahead and
he gave his support, he never really changed his opinion that
it was a daft notion of the minister's.

It was always my bent to exploit special services and
special occasions as a means of boosting congregational life
and encouraging individuals. The big Christian festivals
ought, I believe, always to be made highlights of the worship
and I tried to make them that. Easter is, of course, particularly so, being the heart of the Gospel, but Christmas
runs it pretty close.

It was all the more galling for me, therefore, that I had a number of Christmasses when I was plagued with physical misfortune of one kind or another, despite—thank God—never having a Sunday off through illness in all my ministry.

I awoke one Christmas Eve morning to find that the sore throat I had been carrying for a day or two had developed into such a laryngitis condition that I could barely speak above a whisper and even then only with considerable effort and no little pain. It was quite evident that I could not conduct the Watchnight Service and where on Christmas Eve was I to find a substitute? Most of my ministerial friends had their own watchnight services and, in any case, time was short. The situation was saved by the kindness of the Rev. Nelson Gray. Then heading the religious department of Scottish Television, Nelson, luckily for us, did not have a broadcast to put out that night and for the sake of friendship and the gospel he stepped in to conduct the service—nearly all of it, as my laryngitis prevented me doing any more than giving a few words of welcome and explanation before handing over to him.

Then there was the Christmas when I developed a tooth abscess which came to its climax on Christmas Sunday. I had visited my dentist, Andrew Wright, the previous week when he had diagnosed the abscess in its early stages. The tooth, he judged, would require extraction but with extra church services pending over the next few days, we decided to risk delaying that until after Sunday was past. It was arranged, however, that if I had any real trouble before then I was to get in touch with Andrew immediately, even if it meant telephoning him at home.

Neither of us expected that this emergency course of action would need to be followed but it was. The abscess did not bother me to any extent until late on the Saturday. It began to cause me pain before I went to bed and it brought me suddenly awake in the middle of the night as the pain intensified. By morning one side of my face was swollen into the largest gumboil I had ever seen and the pain was almost unbearable.

As arranged, I rang Andrew and he arranged to see me in his surgery immediately after the morning service which, of course, I had to see through first of all. Warning me that I might not be in the best of condition afterwards for driving, he advised me to have Heather accompany me.

With this somewhat dramatic prelude to it, I went off, gumboil and all, to conduct the worship for Christmas Sunday morning. I realised I could scarcely avoid making some reference to my extremely unsightly appearance and decided to gloss it over as best I could with a hurriedly concocted children's address revolving round my affliction. I hardly knew whether to be gratified or mortified that the children reacted with so much laughter to my admittedly lighthearted references to my condition; but laugh they did. Perhaps they thought it was all pretence, swollen face and all?

When, soon after the service was concluded, Andrew Wright extracted the tooth and drained the abscess, it was for me like a foretaste of heaven to be free from the pain; and I must have looked like a different man in the pulpit in the evening, having lost the huge protuberance that had disfigured my face in the morning.

With these two Christmas experiences behind me I seemed to develop a minor Christmastide complex. More than once as the season approached I would find myself threatened with a sore throat or a heavy cold; and it was always thereafter a great relief to get through the Christmas programme without misadventure.

As we drew near to what was to be my final Christmas in High Carntyne and one that signalled the close of my ministry there, feelings of apprehension about possible physical mishaps were present in abundance, intensified by the fact that my penultimate service, the Christmas Eve Watchnight, was to be televised live by BBC Scotland. In the event all went well. The service, inevitably, was a severe emotional

"The children reacted with so much laughter"

strain since I was not only attempting to lead a nation-wide congregation meaningfully from Christmas Eve into Christmas Day but was at the same time in a sense bringing my long ministry at Carntyne to an end in public view of a large proportion of the country's population.

Not that it was by any means the first television broadcasting I had done from High Carntyne. Amongst other things, some years earlier, with Fiona Kennedy as co-presenter I had introduced several series of programmes entitled 'We've Got A Hymn' which went out in the *Songs Of Praise* slot. These had proved highly popular.

This particular broadcast being a live transmission, the timing was even more important than usual since it was crucial that precisely on midnight I should be in a position to wish all the viewers a happy Christmas without being caught in the middle of a hymn or a prayer. This was successfully accomplished, spot on; and it was now a case of my seeing to it that the service was brought to its conclusion nicely within the allotted time.

I had been advised that we would be taken off the air exactly at twelve minutes past midnight and that I must be finished by then, otherwise we would be cut off abruptly and so spoil our presentation. We were being supported musically by Kilmarnock Concert Brass Band, under the baton of Drew Keachie, with Jim Clark conducting the singing. Our arrangements for the close of the service were that as I began my final short prayer Drew would move from his seat under the pulpit to his rostrum to enable him as soon as I finished the prayer to launch the band into a spirited arrangement of Christmas carols as a finale.

Fortified by the knowledge that my timing at midnight had been immaculate, I was confident that I was still running to time when I embarked on the short closing prayer. To my horror, as well as my surprise, Drew remained rooted to his seat and was still there when I had finished.

'Oh, dear' I thought to myself, 'I must have messed things up and overrun so that we're already off the air. What a pity after it had all gone so well beforehand. Where could I have gone wrong?'

Just then Jim Clark rose to his feet and I waited with my heart in my boots for the explanation and apology I knew he was going to give to the congregation. Instead, he turned to me and said, 'There's a friend of yours, Jim, who could not be here in person tonight but if you look at the monitor screen beside the pulpit you'll see and hear her as she sends you a greeting from Aberdeen.'

When I looked to the screen, it was to see Fiona with her two young children on her lap and to hear her offer me good wishes for Christmas and on my retirement. Ian Mackenzie and May Bowie, the producers of the programme, had set this up as a surprise to me—not even my wife was in on the secret. Surprise it assuredly was, as my face, close to tears, must have made plain, and we *were* still on the air.

I was even closer to tears when, shortly afterwards, the broadcast was brought to a close as planned with Kilmarnock Concert Brass and the Christmas carols. Closer still when Jim Clark called for an expression of appreciation to me for the service and all that lay behind it, and the whole congregation rose to give me a standing ovation.

On the Sunday morning following, the last Sunday of the year and the last service I was to conduct as minister of High Carntyne Church, the tears finally came. As I walked up the centre aisle to the front door after pronouncing the benediction, the packed church stood up as one man or woman and applauded me all the way. I could no longer keep back my tears, tears of joy and sorrow together but especially of gratitude for many blessings, and although I have never stood in that pulpit since that day, the memory remains vivid and moving, humbling and inspiring.

So ended my ministry in High Carntyne, almost 34 years to the day after it began, during which I had preached in it 2,421 sermons, conducted 1,017 baptisms, 1,587 marriages and 2,382 funerals; and, much more important than mere statistics, had, I hope, helped some to find faith, others to rediscover faith and others still to find in their faith the resources required for some crisis that had overtaken them.

Chapter Seven

Some Lessons Carntyne Underlined

HIGH CARNTYNE IMPRESSED UPON me that it is not only large numbers that make the most moving church services. I was fortunate enough to preside over a great many large number occasions in High Carntyne. On many Communion Sundays, for example, I found myself dispensing the sacrament to more than 1,200 worshippers; and yet among the communion services most indelibly imprinted on my memory, are those that took place at the conclusion of our annual elders' conference, when it was just the kirk session and when the simple short service in the church was enhanced by our taking the wine from the olive wood communion cups I had brought from Bethlehem.

For a number of years I was privileged to have first communicant classes that numbered sixty and more. It could not fail to be uplifting for the rest of us when that body of mainly young people stood before the congregation to declare their faith and pledge their allegiance to Jesus Christ and his church. Yet the service of admission that stands out most in my memory involved only one new communicant. Although Agnes Barclay had faithfully attended every one of the classes of preparation which intending new communicants were required to attend, she was unable to be present at the Sunday morning service when the rest of the class were being admitted to full membership. To meet this situation it was agreed that Agnes would be admitted by herself at the

Preparatory Service held on the Sunday evening prior to Communion Sunday.

So it came about that this young girl stood up all by herself in the front of the congregation to make her public profession of Christian faith and to take on board the vows of church membership. I was not alone that night in finding it a singularly inspiring experience to be present when she did. The quiet sincerity of her declaration in face of the congregation and her resolution in making it without the support of others standing beside her struck home to many hearts.

That service also, in its way, emphasised for me the importance of the individual in the sight of God. I rejoiced then and rejoice still at the 'large number' occasions I had in High Carntyne; but I rejoice equally over the many occasions which had a particularly individual aspect, not only those with personal and family connections like my ordaining of my two daughters to the eldership and my baptising of my grandchildren, Martin and Alison, but also those such as the admission of Agnes Barclay. It reminded me of Jesus' parable of the lost sheep and of how when his fellows said, 'Why be concerned? You have ninety-nine sheep safely home,' the shepherd said, 'Yes, but one is missing and that one matters just as much. I must go and find it.'

That message was much in my mind when I conducted the funeral of a certain elderly lady who had died in Lightburn Hospital where I was, and am, chaplain. Although she had family, Margaret had been disowned by them long ago. 'When I went off the rails' she confessed heartbreakingly one day, 'they washed their hands of me.' She had become addicted to the bottle and no doubt had turned difficult to cope with. Now that she was hospitalised, she never had a visitor unless you count the chaplain on his weekly rounds and that is not quite the same.

When she died, there was no known relative to contact regarding funeral arrangements which, consequently, had to be made by the hospital administrator and that is how I came

"Jesus' parable of the lost sheep"

to be called in to conduct the service. There were no mourners except for Sister Reid from her Lightburn ward and myself. The company standing round the grave as her body was committed 'earth to earth, ashes to ashes, dust to dust' was increased to four by virtue of the undertaker and the hearse driver taking up position sympathetically beside us but it was still a very sombre experience, lightened for me only by remembrance of the heavenly shepherd's love for every wandering sheep.

There is another aspect to this, of course, which was also driven home to me in my High Carntyne days, namely that we are not meant, and ought not to try, to live to ourselves alone.

I was playing regularly at the time for Dalziel F.P.'s and was indeed captain of the team. Most of the many High Carntyne weddings took place on Saturday afternoons which would have curtailed my football playing very severely had it not been for the twin facts that the popular hour for High Carntyne weddings was five o'clock and that for the major part of our football season the kick-off time was two o'clock. This usually gave me ample time to complete the match and drive to the church for the wedding.

This arrangement served me very well for a long time but I ran into difficulties one season. As the days lengthened it became customary to start the match a little later and that began to cause problems. Allowing myself ten minutes to change into my street clothes and another fifteen to get to the church meant that to arrive at the church some ten minutes before the wedding was due I had to be off the playing field no later than twenty-five minutes past four. Most weeks this presented no problem but there came a run of several matches which started late, too late to be finished before my essential departure time. I met this circumstance not by standing down but by arranging with the referee to let me know when it was 4.25. I then simply left my colleagues to play out the few minutes remaining without me, no substitutes then. The arrangement appeared to work quite satisfactorily until the day that I took my departure with the score at one goal each, only for the opposing team to score twice in the final minutes. Surprise, surprise, my teammates were inclined to blame me for my desertion.

From then on I did not play unless the match was sure to finish before I needed to leave. Even then it meant that sometimes I had to go to church and wedding without having time to shower. On a wet afternoon this could mean that I had to draw on my trousers over mud-festooned legs and then stand begowned before wedding couple and congregation conscious that a careless movement might send a piece of the now caked mud slithering down my leg to assume an accusing position on the chancel carpet.

For the defence I must plead that I never failed to see to it that my hands and face were scrubbed clean before beginning the wedding service and that I always had time to go home and bathe between wedding and reception. What is more, to the best of my knowledge and belief no morsel of football pitch mud ever did find its way from my legs to the chancel floor, but there may have been the odd instance where it was the proverbial 'close run thing'.

Another truth that was emphasised to me over and over again during my Carntyne ministry was the extent to which any and every one of us is dependent on others.

I was greatly blessed in Newmilns in having an excellent church officer in the person of Robin Gordon. In High Carntyne I had a number of splendidly helpful men occupying that position.

Johnny Kincaid occupied the post in the first few years of my ministry there. He was a beadle of the old school, a real 'minister's man', Sunday by Sunday supervising me into my robes and in his element on a Monday night supervising my weekly Vestry Hour. This was a set and regular time for me to be available at the church for people to consult with me about any matter of concern to them, as well as making arrangements for things like baptisms and marriages. It was usually very busy and was rarely concluded in the prescribed

hour. On one never to be forgotten instance it lasted for
more than three hours. Johnny not only shepherded the
callers in to the vestry when their turn came but entertained
them while they waited by engaging them in conversation
that was liberally salted with his pawky humour.

I noted in the beginning, without ever commenting on it,
that he went out of his way to give me a reminder, usually
the day before, of every wedding that I was to conduct. One
day he saw fit to explain his fastidiousness in this regard.

'You'll maybe be wondering why I always remind you
about the weddings. Well, I'll tell you why. It goes back to
Mr Crichton's time.'

The Rev. Thomas Crichton, a bachelor, had been High
Carntyne's first minister and his memory was greatly, and
deservedly, revered. He had exercised an outstanding ministry and I used to make a point of visiting him annually in his
retirement in Aberdeen and reporting back to the congregation as to how he was faring. I did this until he died at the age
of 96, still with a wealth of affection for High Carntyne in
his heart.

'We had a wedding fixed for four o'clock one afternoon,'
Johnny continued, 'and when it came to ten to four and Mr
Crichton not yet here, I began to get worried. I phoned the
manse but got no reply. Came four o'clock and still no sign
of the minister. Eventually I got a neighbouring minister to
do the wedding but the people were far from pleased and I
was very worried. I'd never known Mr Crichton to miss a
wedding before. However the next day he turned up at the
church hale and hearty. I said to him, quite casually, "Mr
Crichton, where would you happen to be at four o'clock
yesterday?", expecting him to explain, but not a bit of it.'

'Johnny,' he said, 'I'll tell you just where I was at four
o'clock yesterday. It was such a nice day I decided to give
myself a treat and take a drive down the coast. At four
o'clock yesterday afternoon I was sitting in the sun, enjoying
myself, on the seafront at Rhu.'

When I said, 'Did you forget you had a wedding here at

the very time?' I thought he was going to collapse. I've never seen anyone more upset, but the family never forgave him. That's the reason I always give you a reminder, just in case.'

Bill Smith was probably as near being the perfect church officer as anyone could be. He was wholeheartedly committed to the cause of Jesus Christ and his church and totally supported by his wife, Martha, in the execution of his duties. With it all he was wise, sensitive, always ready to help and in addition possessed of a marvellous sense of humour which many a day helped me to set about my work in the pulpit or in the parish with a lighter step and a more joyful heart.

His sense of humour enabled him to cope well with many an unexpected situation which might otherwise have led to heated confrontations. There was, for instance, the wedding service day when, as Bill passed through the church en route to the front door to await the bride's arrival, he observed a guest contentedly puffing away at a cigarette.

'You'll have to put out your cigarette,' Bill said, 'Smoking is not permitted in the church.'

Taken aback the guest protested, 'How was I to know that? I don't see any NO SMOKING signs.'

'That's true,' countered Bill, 'but neither do we have any signs saying DON'T THROW ROTTEN EGGS AT THE MINISTER. Some things we expect people to know, and not to smoke in the church is one of them.'

With that rejoinder a potentially inflammatory situation was damped down. It was a pointed hint to me, however, that there may well be times when we who are regular church-goers assume too much acquaintance with our procedures on the part of those who are not.

Admittedly there are times and occasions when even the person in the pulpit may not be too sure of the correct procedure to adopt. When, for instance, someone takes ill or has a fainting turn during the sermon, an occurrence which, unsurprisingly in view of the large attendances, was not uncommon in High Carntyne. (It was never, I trust, brought on by the sermon itself and I hasten to assure you that it is quite untrue that on one occasion an afflicted lady on being asked, 'Are you conscious?', she replied 'Unfortunately, yes, for I can still hear him.')

It was always a problem deciding whether to stop or to carry on. The important question was how ill the individual was. If it was only a slight indisposition, for me to halt the sermon in mid flow was likely by thus focusing attention on the incident to cause embarrassment and so increase discomfort. If, on the other hand, the person appeared to be more seriously affected, it seemed clear that the best thing to do was to suspend the service temporarily and allow those who were giving assistance to concentrate on doing just that.

So far as old Mrs Brough was concerned there was never any dilemma. The service simply had to stop while she was carried bodily out of the church, an event which took place with almost unfailing regularity every quarterly communion service. Mrs Brough would insist on coming to communion dressed in her best, her fur coat, even though the church was invariably warm, and insisted also in sitting not at the end of a row but right in the middle. When, as so often happened, she succumbed to the heat and passed out, inevitably a commotion ensued. She had to be taken out of the church and this could be done only by carrying her out after clearing sufficient space in her immediate vicinity. This kind of operation made it impossible to contemplate proceeding simultaneously with the worship.

Mrs Brough was, of course, on my list of regular home visits because of her age and her frail state of health. One day soon after the removal from church scene had been played out once more, I summoned up the courage to raise the matter with her, knowing that the commotion she caused, albeit inadvertently, spoiled the communion service to a great extent for many of the congregation. I was as tactful as I knew how. After referring to the recent episode and being assured by her that she was none the worse for it, I ventured to say, 'Perhaps if you are not feeling quite up to the mark on a Communion Sunday you should just stay at home. The

Lord knows, as we all do, where your heart lies but we don't want you to risk making yourself really ill.'

I could see her drawing herself up to her full height of five feet little or nothing before she said, 'I would like nothing better than to die in the church. In fact, you might say it's my ambition and I'm going to keep coming, no matter how I feel.'

And so it continued, with a general acceptance of the fact that many a Sunday morning service, Communion particularly, was likely to include the ceremonial carrying out of the collapsed Mrs Brough almost as part of the liturgy.

Her ambition, however, was never realised. As time passed and she became still older and frailer, she became unfit to live alone. Her only surviving relative lived some distance away and he arranged for her to be accommodated in a private nursing home in Uddingston. With her lack of relatives and lack, too, of personal friends since she had always been a bit of a loner, I am afraid that Mrs Brough had few visits from outside except for myself. She did not, after all, die in church and little more than a handful were present at her funeral—a scarcely needed lesson that none of us can plan our destiny with precision.

A lesson of a different kind that came my way in High Carntyne was to the effect that trusting people are easily 'conned' and at the same time that the downfall of a confidence trickster may well be the result of over-confidence.

One evening I had a telephone call from a member of the congregation. This, I may say, was many years ago, long before Glasgow entered into the smokeless zone era.

'Mr Martin' the caller began 'I've just had a young woman at my door to say that a few tons of coal have been made available to you for selling cheap to selected members of the congregation. She said she was calling on your behalf to offer a ton to me. I was happy to accept the offer and was happy to give her the £4 she said needed to be paid in advance. Now that she has gone, I'm feeling a little uneasy. It's not like you not to come yourself and I want you to reassure me that she was genuine.'

Unfortunately she was not genuine. I knew nothing about this supposed cheap coal bounty. The young woman's story was a complete fabrication and I soon discovered, on making some enquiries, that a number of others had parted with money to the same confidence trickster. In an endeavour to prevent further victims I gave a warning from the pulpit on the Sunday morning about the plausible young woman and the trick she was playing.

From eleven o'clock onwards that night the manse phone hardly stopped ringing as newspaper after newspaper called to enquire about the mysterious 'woman in red' who had been reaping a harvest amongst my congregation. Stuart M'Cartney, a young reporter in the congregation, had seen the announcement I had made as providing a good story for his paper and had phoned it in. Now that his paper's first edition was on the streets, a number of other papers wanted to use the story, too. Hence the busy phone and the fact that most of the daily papers carried the story next morning.

When I learned of the extensive press coverage I felt a great sense of relief in regard to other potential victims. The woman, whoever she was, obviously would drop her scheme now that it had been made so public. It was, therefore, with great surprise that I answered the telephone the next day to hear another of my congregation tell me that she had just had a visit from a young woman with the selfsame story that I had quoted in church on Sunday. My caller had directed the fraudster to a friend of hers two streets away who was 'sure to be interested' while she herself hastened to telephone me.

Her quick thinking paid off. I contacted the police, a squad car was sent to the friend's address and arrived in nice time to apprehend the young woman in the middle of her story. I never discovered whether she had not read the newspapers or merely hoped that she could continue to get away with her fraud despite the publicity.

She was one of many examples I came across in my High

Carntyne ministry of human frailty and even wickedness. These caused me no little depression and even personal hurt, especially when I came up against duplicity, false friendship and maliciousness as was sometimes the case. Much, much more, however, thank God, I encountered goodness and kindness, loyal friendship and helpfulness, and a large volume of graciousness as well; and these are things that make for good memories.

On one memorable occasion the graciousness encountered was displayed by a fellow minister. The occasional minister, it must be confessed, is not always as disposed to graciousness as might be expected. For instance, a minister I know who had spent half a lifetime in a certain parish was succeeded by a man who expressed the view that his predecessor ought not to have any continuing friendly contact with any of his former members as this would mean a maintenance of the pastoral link and he even actively discouraged such contact.

The knowledge that some can be like that makes all the more precious to me the graciousness I now recall. Nearly a year after my induction to High Carntyne, another minister approached me after the Presbytery meeting one night. After introducing himself, he went on to say, 'I was a candidate for High Carntyne and very keen to get it. It was, therefore, a big disappointment to me when they called you. But now I rejoice because I hear of the fine job you are doing there and it is clear to me that you were and are God's man for it. God bless you.' And he shook my hand with patent warmth and sincerity. I was touched and moved; and ever afterwards had the highest regard for Thomson Revel. I thank God that I have met so many of similar stamp, living proofs that when given the chance, the gospel of Jesus Christ really works.

Chapter Eight

Life After High Carntyne

ALL THE TIME I WAS MINISTER of High Carntyne there was life for me outside the congregation and parish, lots of it.

I was a school chaplain, first of all at Gartcraig Junior Secondary directly across Carntyne Square from the church. For girls who had not gained enough marks in the dreaded 'quali' to advance them to senior secondary education, Gartcraig is firmly lodged in my memory as a school of outstanding quality. In my experience of it, it had two gifted headmistresses in Miss Lindsay and Miss Stobo, backed by an exceptional staff. The philosophy controlling the operation of the school was that every girl had at least one talent that was worth developing and their philosophy was proved sound over and over again. So much so that to this day, many years after it ceased to be, I am approached by former pupils who express their gratitude for their years at Gartcraig.

When Smithycroft Senior Secondary was built, outside my parish but not far away, Gartcraig was incorporated in it and I was invited to be chaplain there. Here I continued, as with Gartcraig, to have a short weekly service of worship, no longer, because of the distance, in the church but in the new school's fine assembly hall. In Smithycroft I continued also to have splendid support from successive head teachers and of it, too, I retain many happy memories.

There was, also, my chaplaincy to Collins the Publishers;

my chaplaincy to Lightburn Hospital; my chaplaincy (unofficial) to Motherwell Football Club; my chaplaincy on a number of school cruises—on Dunera, Devonia, Uganda, Nevasa; my chaplaincy on many Holy Land pilgrimages; my chaplaincy and keynote speaker role at a number of conferences, notably those involving American military personnel in Europe and the United Kingdom.

I will not trouble the reader by saying any more meantime about that life outside High Carntyne; but before I bring to a close this particular rag-bag of ministerial reminiscences I want to put on record that there has also been life *after* High Carntyne, even in retirement, and a good life, too. Since retiring I have had scarcely one free Sunday. Following five Sundays of pulpit supply I was locum tenens for more than a year in Airdrie: Broomknoll, then occupied a similar position in Wishaw: Thornlie before becoming locum at Motherwell: North.

For those first weeks after retirement I supplied the pulpit in the linked charges of Twechar and Banton; and retain fond memories of that sojourn. It gave me at the same time a salutary reminder of how hard it is for some of our smaller church communities to keep the flag flying and of how often they deserve the highest praise for managing to do it as bravely as they do.

My wife and I went along early to Twechar that first morning, not being familiar either with the area or with the church. On a bleak mid-winter day we made the journey in some trepidation. The interim-moderator had been on the telephone the day before to warn me that because of a boiler failure there would be no heating possible in the church and that the service therefore would be held in the hall where auxiliary heaters were available. Forewarned we came heavily clad and just as well.

On arrival I was informed that the service would, after all, be in the church since workmen had begun work in the hall the day before to convert it for use as a playgroup centre and had rendered it unusable for the time being. The church, a large and once beautiful building, the legacy of more affluent times, was extremely cold and I determined that the service must be as bright and as cheerful as it could possibly be made. 'Is the organist here yet?' I enquired, 'I would like to discuss the praise list with him or her.'

'Well' said the session clerk who, I had discovered to my delight, was Bill Calder who had been one of my Holy Land group in 1983, 'we don't have a regular organist but there is a lady who plays when she comes but so far she has not turned up today.'

Nor did she appear at all and in the end my wife agreed to play, despite not only lacking her normal organ shoes but having her feet encased in her snow boots. What made things worse was that damp and lack of heat had badly affected a once fine instrument so that some of the stops and some of the keys no longer functioned, and the congregation numbered only 27. (I could not help thinking of the no doubt apocryphal tale of the bishop with a reputation as a boring preacher who was conducting worship one Sunday in a church in his diocese. The attendance was abysmally low and after the service the bishop said to the vicar, rather pompously, 'Did you tell them that I was to be preaching today?' 'I certainly did not' replied the vicar, 'but when I find out who did, he'll get a piece of my mind.')

In spite of all, we made, I think, a really joyful noise in praise of the Lord; but I was unable to avoid thinking ruefully of High Carntyne which I had so recently left and of its hundreds sitting at that same moment in warmth and comfort, to a large extent taking it all pretty much for granted just as I myself had done for so many years. My heart reached out then, as it does still, to all those devoted Christian men and women who strive against many odds to maintain a faithful witness; and because of them I try all the more to count my own blessings.

Having, despite the adverse external circumstances, managed to praise the Lord and proclaim his word, we left Twechar with the assurance ringing in our ears that next week we would be more comfortable. If the boiler was not repaired by then we would certainly worship in the hall. After a quick cup of tea, we raced to Banton some eight miles distant where we found a smaller but warmer church building, an organist, a somewhat larger attendance and another little band of dedicated Christians fighting a good fight in difficult circumstances.

The following Sunday we did indeed worship in the hall in Twechar, with their own organist playing the piano, and received a solemn promise from the Property Convener that the boiler would be functioning by the next week. On Saturday morning I received a jubilant phone call to say that the boiler was restored and had been running all through Friday night to make sure. I was to have no further anxiety about the wintry weather and the low outside temperature. The church was sure to be comfortably warm on the morrow.

When we arrived on the Sunday morning it was to be given the sad news that a fire had erupted in the boiler house overnight—vandalism was strongly suspected—and once again, despite all the repair work that had been put in, the heating system was out of commission. One or two portable heaters had been assembled and the service went ahead in the church, partly because a baby was to be baptised and the mother, understandably, was anxious that the sacrament be celebrated there.

My last Sunday there, before taking up the post of locum tenens at Airdrie's Broomknoll Church, was one of some personal gratification. Over the weeks the numbers had shown a steady, if unspectacular, increase and on this final Sunday the total was 55. That was incidental. The chief cause for rejoicing was that the boiler was repaired, the heating was restored and the church was warm.

It was with genuine regret that we took farewell of Twechar and Banton and the fine people we had come to know in both places; but this was more than compensated by the happiness in store at Broomknoll. I rediscovered, as I had first discovered in Newarthill all those years ago, that in many respects the locum's lot is a very happy one. It can provide so much of the 'job-satisfaction' without most of the disappointments and let-downs that tend to come the way of the average minister in full charge. He has the satisfaction, often intense, of preaching the gospel and may even have the unsurpassed joy of seeing response to his preaching, the satisfaction of bringing comfort to sick and sorrowing, the satisfaction of helping the troubled—and all this without the final responsibility of all that goes on in the congregation. In some ways I was able to appreciate the situation even more than in my Newarthill period simply by virtue of the fact that now, for more than forty years, I had been the man with whom 'the buck' stopped and here, joy of joys, it no longer belonged on my desk.

In Broomknoll, although involved only to the limited extent that is a locum's remit, I nevertheless, just as in my full ministries at Newmilns and Carntyne, encountered the whole range of human joy and human sorrow in the experiences of those to whom I was attempting to minister, with more than a little added poignancy at times.

For instance, my introduction to Broomknoll was my attendance at the congregation's Annual Business Meeting. The entertainment which followed the business was compered in very witty fashion by John Kerr, whom I found to be the life and soul of many a Broomknoll function in the ensuing months, and during those months I also had the privilege of conducting his youngest daughter's wedding. That introduction was in February 1987. In May 1988 I had the sad task of conducting John Kerr's funeral service immediately prior to my going off to the Holy Land to lead a pilgrimage. The night after my return I found myself compering a church concert which had been originally scheduled to be compered by John. It was not surprising that not one of his Broomknoll friends could face the heartrending task of standing that night where he had been intending to stand; and even I, a mere bird of passage, found it far from easy. Less than a year later his wife, Margaret, was also dead of cancer.

Through all their grief the Christian hope of the life everlasting shone like a beacon in the darkness for the Kerr family and their friends; and I felt it a privilege to be a witness to it.

In the case of Lana Johnstone I saw darkness turn to light. Four years of age, she was suddenly stricken with renal failure. Rushed into Glasgow's Sick Children's Hospital, she was given little or no hope of survival. Her parents sat at her bedside continually, hoping for a miracle but fearing the worst. When I went to see her in her hospital bed, it was a sight calculated to pierce the hardest heart to look on her so pale and obviously so ill, all the more so when she mustered a wan little smile and whispered, 'Hello, Dr Martin,' and went on to say, 'and how is Bobby?' (Bobby being my little friend whose exploits I was in the habit of relating to the children on Sunday mornings.)

I wondered if I would ever see Lana alive again but when I went back a day or two later she was marvellously improved, 'Lana' I exclaimed delightedly, 'You are looking so much better today.'

'Yes, Dr Martin' she replied with all her former four-year old assurance, 'And I am feeling much better, too.'

It was a matter of great rejoicing not only to her family but to all the congregation that her improvement continued and that a full recovery was made.

Broomknoll, too, had its 'characters', some of whom I got to know quite well. On my first visit to Meadowside House I was warned that the oldest of the elderly ladies I was to see there was, at the age of 90, usually quite confused and that I should be prepared for a rather nonsensical conversation. I was not in the least surprised, therefore, when on introducing myself to her, Miss Grubb said, 'Oh, I know you all right. I have often been at your church.' But when she went on to mention High Carntyne by name and to tell me of the family in my congregation that she used to visit, I realised

"Lana, you are looking so much better today"

that, confused as she may well have been at most times, on this occasion, perhaps through recognising a face from the past, she was as lucid as could be.

That was one first visit that remains firmly in my mind. Another was the one I made to Mrs Wood. At the age of 87 she had had a hip replacement and, although back home from hospital, was housebound and not very mobile. I had been advised that it would take a little time for her to answer the door and I was not surprised to have to wait after ringing the bell.

It was, however, not Mrs Wood who opened the door but one of the three friends who happened to be visiting. Not only were they visiting, they were entertaining her by making up a foursome at whist, as I saw from the cards lying on the table before them. They appeared ever so slightly flustered at the entrance of this hitherto unknown minister and so, after enquiring after Mrs Wood's health, I attempted to put them at their ease by remarking to her with feeble jocularity, 'I'm glad you managed to get the money out of sight before I came in. It would have been awful if I'd caught you gambling on my first visit.'

It was only when I made my next call on her that Mrs Wood confessed that they had in fact been playing for pennies and that the delay in answering the door was to enable the coins to be scooped up and hidden!

One precious memory of Broomknoll is of the continuing kindness of the incoming minister to the departed locum. At the very outset of his ministry, I had to approach him for his permission to conduct a marriage which had been arranged long before his coming, where the bridegroom, an Australian, was known to me but not to him and for that reason among others the bride's family were most anxious that I should perform the ceremony, if at all possible.

'Of course' was John Young's immediate response, 'I am grateful for all you have done here to strengthen the congregation and you will always be welcome here in any capacity. Go ahead and do the wedding with my blessing.'

I am happy to say that I met a similar attitude of goodwill on the part of the incoming ministers when I handed over to them at the end of my next two locum spells and these, too, are full of rich memories of events and people.

I discovered, for instance, to my great delight that my little friend Bobby became a favourite of the children in Thornlie just as of the children of Carntyne and Airdrie. So much so that when I left Thornlie on the advent of the new minister, the session clerk, John Irvine, presented me with a large box of jelly babies which 'Bobby had requested him to hand over on his behalf since he knew I had a liking for them.' Mind you, I was not too sure how to take the notice printed on the box stating FREE INSIDE. MOTHER-WELL FOOTBALL TEAM. And after I took leave of North Motherwell, the minister, Alison Paul, happily restored to health, proceeded to sell large quantities of my book of Bobby stories to young and older members of the congregation. This was a noble, even sacrificial, action since I know she had originally planned, using that book, to continue the Bobby stories for a time—no trace here of the envy of their colleagues which is reputed to taint some ministers!

It was while I was at Thornlie that I came within a whisker of notching up another first, and one not to be desired. In the two thousand or so marriage services I have conducted, none has ever had to be cancelled owing to the illness of the bride or the bridegroom. But it nearly happened when Dorothy Ramsay was married to Billy Jackson the Friday after Christmas 1989.

I had spoken to Dorothy after morning service the preceding Sunday which was Christmas Eve. As she left me she said she would be coming to the Watchnight service that night but when she failed to appear, I thought little of it, assuming that, with the wedding so near, something else had intervened that required attention. The truth of the matter was that Dorothy who had been feeling perfectly all right earlier in the day was suddenly laid low with chicken-pox

LIFE AFTER HIGH CARNTYNE   121

which, of course, generally hits an adult much harder than it does a child.

For a day or two it looked as if Dorothy would have to postpone the wedding, but an improvement in her condition, allied to her strong determination, meant that, after all and in spite of the bleak wintry afternoon it turned out to be, she walked up the aisle at the appointed time. What is more, a liberal and skilful application of white powder ensured that her generous supply of spots was hidden from view.

My wife and I were exceedingly happy in our temporary liaison with the people of Thornlie, just as we had been with those of Broomknoll; and the same proved true in our much shorter period at North Motherwell. All of these experiences underlined for me what Newarthill had indicated long ago that the locum's life is an excellent example of having the best of two worlds, the joy of the job and freedom from most of its hassle.

In every locum I engaged in, the richness of my memories, as with my full ministries at Newmilns and Carntyne, is due in largest measure to the many splendid people I got to know. Not all, mark you, belonged to the 'marvellous' category. I could tell you about some who were not so pleasant specimens but, as with most ministers, I have a host of glad memories of people who showed themselves to be truly committed Christians and loyal friends to boot.

In each locum, admittedly, there were some disappointing, even infuriating, experiences. On my third Sunday in North Motherwell, for instance, I had two baptisms to conduct at the beginning of the morning service. My own preferred practice is to have the baptisms towards the close of the service but this other was the usual way of things in North Motherwell and the interim-moderator had arranged things accordingly. He had also arranged for the baptismal parties to see me in good time before the service was due to begin in order to confirm the procedure with them and also attend to the paperwork involved. One party arrived well beforehand but the other had been given up as 'no shows' when they panted into the premises.

'We thought you weren't coming' I said, 'You were supposed to be here at least fifteen minutes ago.'

'We got held up' said the father, with no further explanation, far less apology.

'It would have been better' I said 'if I'd had time to talk to you a little before we went into the church and also if we'd had time to fill up the register and the certificate but that will have to wait until after the service. The men will be staying in for the remainder of the service, although the ladies will be leaving with the baby after the baptism.'

And so we proceeded. I was mildly surprised when the father and godfather walked out of the church along with the church officer as he escorted, mother, godmother and baby out of the church but concluded they were simply seeing the others off before returning to the church. The church officer, however, came back in alone and the others failed to appear. When I went to the door to greet the exiting congregation after the service, I asked the church officer what had happened.

'They just refused to come back in with me' he replied 'and went off with the others.'

I was disappointed to say the least but my disappointment was exceeded by my surprise when I returned to the vestry to find the men sitting there waiting for me to have the certificates signed.

'Why didn't you come back into the service as you were expected to do?' I asked.

'Oh' responded the father, 'We didn't know that we could go back in.'

I was rendered almost speechless—almost!

Even in the semi-retirement life of a locum tenens there sometimes are pinpricks of that nature; but pinpricks they are seen to be in the wider context of the faithfulness and the enthusiasm, the goodwill and the gratitude, the graciousness and the responsiveness of so many. The disappointments are as nothing compared with the rewards that come the minister's way in terms of his awareness of people helped, of lives repaired, of souls redeemed—even when that awareness comes, as it often may, long after the particular event.

I recall, for example, that one of the many letters I received after my televised farewell service from High Carntyne expressed the writer's gratitude for the fact that my pastoral ministrations on the occasion of a family bereavement had been the means of saving her faith, and perhaps her life. The occasion was one I had long forgotten and what I had done was no more than what most ministers are doing week in week out. But such sentiments as were expressed in that letter, and what lay behind them, are what make the ministry the marvellous job it is. Surely the best in the world.

Enjoying my retirement as I do, I cannot help at the same time feeling envious of those who are just embarking on their ministries in the church. I would gladly be starting all over again!

It's You Minister

by James Martin

Well known as a TV and radio broadcaster, football playing chaplain, and writer, James Martin recounts his true-life stories which make fascinating reading for anyone who longs to know what being a minister is *really* like.

Here, too, are many of the people who have made the author's life so rewarding, with both funny encounters and also sad experiences to share.

Readers, whether church folks or not, will enjoy James Martin's 'tales of the ministry'—all the humour and the hurts which go with the job of the man in the dog collar.

ISBN 0-948643-07-2